THEORY
FOR
RELIGIOUS
STUDIES

theory4

A book series from
ROUTLEDGE

THEORY
FOR
RELIGIOUS
STUDIES

William E. Deal and Timothy K. Beal

ROUTLEDGE New York • London

Published in 2004 by
Routledge
270 Madison Ave.
New York, NY 10016

Theory 4: a book series from Routledge

www.routledge-ny.com
Published in Great Britain by
Routledge
2 Park Square
Milton Park, Abingdon
Oxon, Ox14 4RN, U.K.
www.routledge.co.uk

Routledge is an imprint of the Taylor & Francis Group.
© 2004 by Taylor & Francis Books, Inc.

Printed in the United States of America on acid free paper.

10 9 8 7 6 5 4 3 2 1

Library of Congress Cataloging-in-Publication Data

Deal, William E.
    Theory for religious studies / William E. Deal & Timothy K. Beal.
       p. cm.—(Theory4)
    ISBN 0-415-96638-8 (hardcover : alk. paper)—ISBN 0-415-96639-6 (pbk. : alk. paper)
    1. Religion—Study and teaching—Methodology. I. Beal, Timothy K. (Timothy
Kandler), 1963–   . II. Title. III. Series.
    BL41.D46 2004
    200'.71—dc22
                                                        2004013888

DEDICATION

for
Lisa Robertson
and
Clover Reuter Beal

CONTENTS

ACKNOWLEDGMENTS

We are grateful to many colleagues, students, and friends for help and encouragement. Together we want to thank, Christine Fergus and Nikki Krempasky, who provided invaluable research assistance and Julie Digiantonio and Matt Snyder, who edited the final text. Although we cannot mention them all by name, we also wish to acknowledge the many conversations in and out of the classroom with students in several of our religion courses at Case Western Reserve University, especially "Introduction to the Study of Religion," "Interpreting Buddhist Texts," "Religion and Horror," "Ritual," "Religion and Postmodernism," and "Senior Seminar." If those students are our ideal readers, then others have been our ideal critics, for whom we are equally grateful, in particular, Vincent Leitch, William Germano, and Gilad Foss.

Bill thanks Tim Murphy, James Flanagan, Norman Havens, Thomas Wilson, Joseph Parker, Karen Smyers, John Solt, Jeremy Giddings, and Brian Ruppert for many illuminating conversations about theory, culture, and religion over the years. He dedicates this book to Lisa Robertson with gratitude for enduring his theoretical mood swings, for providing intellectual and emotional encouragement, and loving support.

Tim thanks Tod Linafelt, Brent Plate, and other members of the Tel Mac Theory Lunch and Praxis Breakfast, for continued conversation and e-conversation about critical theory and religion. Above all and as ever, he is deeply indebted to his best and dearest colleague, reader, and partner, Clover Reuter Beal, to whom he dedicates this book.

INTRODUCTION

Theory for Religious Studies—Who Needs It?

What is theory and why is it important for religious studies?

Theory, from the Greek *theoria*, which means "a viewing" or "spectacle," offers a way of seeing. A theory is something like a conceptual lens, a pair of spectacles, that you use to frame and focus what you're looking at. It is a tool for discerning, deciphering, and making sense.

One central question that animates the academic study of religion is "What is religion?" Although the answers to this question are diverse, any answer constitutes a de facto theory of religion, that is, an idea of religion that is used to make sense of various beliefs and practices we call religious. Religious studies *is* theory; it is the myriad conceptual tools used to "see" religion.

It has become clear over the past two centuries that the academic study of religion has no GUT, that is, no Grand Unifying Theory that brings into sharp focus all things religious. And it never will. Every theory frames and focuses our attention on some things while leaving other things outside the frame or out of focus. Thus, religious studies is always in search of new theories that might open up new ways of seeing and interpreting religion.

In recent decades, religion scholars have moved beyond their traditional disciplinary boundaries in search of new theoretical perspectives by which to interpret religion. Theories of culture, history, language, and gender that were unfamiliar to most religionists in the past are today reframing and refocusing how we see religion. As a result, the canon of theories and methods important to the academic study of religion has been dramatically transformed and expanded. This situation makes religious studies an exciting and vibrant academic field. Yet it also presents religion students and teachers with significant challenges. These new theories ask innovative questions and reveal novel possibilities for studying and interpreting religion, but they are often difficult to understand. *Theory for Religious Studies* provides concise introductions to the theories of the most prominent scholars outside religious studies whose work has proven important within the field.

We wrote this book with three audiences in mind. First, it is for undergraduate students in courses on theory and methodology for the academic study of religion. Although there are excellent introductions to traditional theories of religion (covering, among others, Tylor, Durkheim, Weber, Otto, Eliade, Turner, and Geertz), there has not been a corresponding introduction to newer theoretical perspectives treated here.

Second, this book is for graduate students. Not only will it serve master's or doctoral students seeking theoretical frameworks for thesis or dissertation research, but it will also prove useful as they prepare for a career in teaching.

Finally, *Theory for Religious Studies* is intended for teachers and scholars of religion who need a resource to help them introduce students to contemporary theoretical perspectives and who are themselves interested in how these perspectives might speak more directly to religious studies.

Genesis

This book had its genesis in the classroom. It has been our experience in teaching courses in academic religious studies that students often find traditional theoretical perspectives on religion relatively easy to grasp. For instance, the modernist notion, identified especially with Durkheim and Eliade, that a sacred/profane dichotomy is foundational to understanding religion poses little difficulty for most students. This is due in part to the fact that the idea of a sacred/profane split has found its way into our "commonsense" understandings about the nature of religion. That there exists a fundamental division between the sacred and the profane seems obvious. Indeed, most Americans would not find it odd to think that some aspects of one's life are lived in the secular, profane world, while other aspects—times of worship and prayer, for example—are set apart as sacred. Further, the binary opposition of sacred and profane parallels other binary oppositions that shape our worldview, such as church and state, right and wrong, and good and evil.

Introducing less commonsensical—often contemporary and explicitly "postmodern"—theories and perspectives is another matter. The conceptual effort required to understand these theories and viewpoints can be quite great. Besides the fact that they often seem to fly in the face of logic, these theories do not necessarily directly address issues of religion and religious phenomena. They also introduce new terms and concepts—such as discourse, representation, subjectivity, gender, ideology, embodiment, and culture—that are unfamiliar to many students and do not at first glance seem to have much to do with religion.

Other than their fashionability, what do these theories offer to the student of religion?

The theories introduced in this book offer fresh perspectives that move us beyond traditional approaches to religion. They raise questions that illuminate the nature of religious practice and thought in ways that require us to see religious phenomena not as isolated texts and events, but as interconnected aspects of culture that both impact and are impacted by the social, the political, the economic, and other human practices.

In its formative years, the study of religion struggled to legitimate itself as a distinct academic discipline alongside other humanities disciplines. The existence of academic departments of religion at most colleges and universities today is one sign of its success in gaining credibility within the academy. Yet the questions asked and perspectives taken by the founders of academic religious studies now seem dated, based on the intellectual assumptions and interests of previous generations. In general, the humanities and social sciences have taken up new questions and perspectives that embrace both interdisciplinarity and contemporary critical and cultural theory. In 1965 one would have likely read, among others, Mircea Eliade and Wilfred Cantwell Smith for guidance on how to study religion academically. Eliade and Smith are still required reading for students and scholars of religion, but the discipline has been confronted by new theoretical ideas and challenges, and these, too, must be taken into careful account. To this end, *Theory for Religious Studies* introduces some of the key thinkers and ideas that are currently having considerable impact on thinking and writing in the humanities and social sciences generally and in the academic study of religion specifically. Students of religion must enter into dialogue with these new perspectives or risk becoming irrelevant, unable to address the questions and issues concerning religion and culture that are now animating the academy.

Conversations

This book is not only a guide about how theory since the 1960s has transformed the landscape of academic religious studies, but also an invitation to join in the conversation—regardless of the theoretical stance one adopts.

The contemporary theoretical perspectives introduced in this book did not emerge miraculously, *ex nihilo*, from the solitary minds of their authors. They were developed in conversation with those who preceded them. In this regard, four theoretical predecessors are particularly important: Sigmund Freud, Karl Marx, Friedrich Nietzsche, and Ferdinand Saussure. Together, these four constitute a common context for theoretical discourse since the mid-twentieth century. Indeed, their concepts and questions continue to set the agenda for contemporary theory. Whether one embraces them or not, one must have a basic understanding of their contributions. Therefore, this book begins with a section on these four predecessors to contemporary theory.

Just as the theorists introduced in this book were engaged in dialogue with their own theoretical predecessors, we invite today's students of religion to be in conversation with the theories and theorists described here. Whether one ultimately declares oneself a Kristevan or Foucauldian or Lacanian—or, for that matter, a Marxist or Freudian or Nietzschean or Saussurean—it is important to attend to the questions these thinkers raise. What happens to our view of religion, for instance, when we question the nature of language? Does language represent a natural correspondence between word and external referent, or, as structuralists would argue, is language a semiotic system in which the linguistic sign is both arbitrary and based on difference? The point is that these critical modes of inquiry allow us to see religion in ways not considered by traditional theories of religion.

How to Use This Book

This book is designed to be useful. We assume that most readers will not read it from cover to cover, but will go to it for help with particular theorists and theories. The four predecessors introduced in the opening section are presented in alphabetical order by last name, as are the twenty-five entries in the main section. Every entry in the book has three main parts: a list of Key Concepts, the main body of the text, and a Further Reading section.

At the beginning of each entry is a short bulleted list of Key Concepts that we have identified as particularly important for students of religion to understand. These concepts are listed in the order of their appearance in the main text.

The main body of each entry begins with a brief biographical sketch. In the discussion that follows, Key Concepts are highlighted where they are first explained. Thus a reader interested in one particular Key Concept can quickly scan the entry for the discussion of it. We also offer some possible implications for religious studies. We do not indicate all the possible implications, however, as if that were possible. To return to our spectacles metaphor, these theories provide us with new lenses through which to interpret religion. We fully expect that others will discover new and surprising ways of applying them.

Finally, each entry has a Further Reading section that includes two subsections: first, a "By" subsection listing those primary texts we consider particularly important for the study of religion; second, an "About" subsection listing texts about the theorist as well as texts on religion that include a significant discussion of the theorist or application of the theorist's ideas. Within each of these subsections, one or two key texts are indicated with asterisks. We recommend these as starting points for further reading.

This book suggests multiple possible ways that we might see religion. Although the theorists we explore here are sometimes difficult to understand on first contact, we believe that they are well worth the effort. Our goal has been to provide initial access to their work, to explain their key concepts, and to give direction for further study. As readers move beyond our short introductions to the primary texts, we fully expect that they will develop more complex and subtle understandings of the potential contributions of these theorists to the academic study of religion than we present here. Happy theorizing.

PREDECESSORS

SIGMUND FREUD

Key Concepts

- psychoanalysis
- unconscious
- repression
- Oedipus Complex
- illusion

Sigmund Freud (1856–1939) was born to a Jewish family in Freiburg, Germany. The Freuds moved to Vienna when he was four. Throughout his school years, he was an outstanding student. He graduated with distinction from gymnasium in 1878 and took his medical degree at the University of Vienna in 1881. In 1885 he won a modest medical scholarship that allowed him to travel to Paris, where he worked under the great Jean-Martin Charcot (1825–1893) at the Salpêtrière hospital. Freud was fascinated with Charcot's work on hysteria, which he treated as a disease, and his use of hypnotism to reproduce symptoms of hysteria in his patients. In 1886 Freud began his practice as a physician in Vienna, where his focus was likewise on nervous disorders. Vienna remained his home until 1938, when he was forced to flee Austria for England following the Nazi *Anschluss*. He died in London.

Freud was the founder of **psychoanalysis**. In a 1922 essay for a general audience, Freud provided three interrelated definitions of psychoanalysis: (1) a discipline focused on investigating the unconscious, (2) a therapeutic method for treating nervous disorders, and (3) a growing body of research data (two encyclopedia articles). Together these three definitions provide a helpful introduction to Freud's work.

First, Freud defines psychoanalysis as an academic discipline whose aim is to investigate and analyze otherwise inaccessible mental processes, which Freud describes as the workings of the **unconscious**. The unconscious is, most simply put, the nonconscious part of the mind. As such, it affects conscious thought and behavior but is not directly accessible for interpretation. Freud's innovation in psychology was not the discovery of the unconscious per se (others, including Nietzsche, had written about it), but rather the means to access and interpret it. He did so through analysis of slips of the tongue, jokes, and above all dreams, which he called the "royal road" to the unconscious. Dreams, Freud believed, represent fulfillments of unconscious wishes and desires that the conscious mind censors because they are socially taboo or a threat to the integrity of the self. For Freud, the content of the unconscious is essentially those drives that are inadmissible to the conscious self and are therefore forced out of consciousness through mechanisms of **repression**. These include drives and memories related to the "primal scene" (childhood recollection of seeing her/his parents having sex) as well as taboo desires related to the Oedipus Complex. Although repressed, they inevitably resurface in dreams, "Freudian slips," and other forms of expression.

The **Oedipus Complex** is particularly important to Freud's understanding of human consciousness and the origin of nervous disorders. The name comes from the Greek legend of Oedipus, who unwittingly kills his father, marries his mother, and then blinds himself when he realizes what he has done. For Freud, the Oedipus Complex concerns the young child's attraction to the parent of the opposite sex and jealousy of the parent of the same sex. Although girls and boys experience this attraction and negotiate this complex differently, in both cases the goal is to transition from jealousy of the same-sex parent to identification with her or him. Freud believes that the Oedipus Complex is a universal event, and the failure to negotiate it successfully is the primary cause of nervous disorders.

Freud's second definition of psychoanalysis is as a therapeutic method for treating nervous disorders. The method largely involves uncensored, free association by the patient (analysand), who lies on a couch while the analyst sits behind her or him and listens for subtle manifestations to the unconscious processes that are the source of the neurosis. The primary medium of psychoanalysis, then, is the spoken word. Indeed, one of Freud's early patients aptly characterized psychoanalysis as the "talking cure." It does not take words at face value, but it sifts through the language of the conscious mind for traces of the unconscious. The speaking human subject is approached as a divided subject, a site of conflict between conscious and unconscious drives that do not come together into a single, integrated, whole self. In this respect some have suggested that Freud's approach bears some influence from the Jewish rabbinic methods of interpretation, which approach the biblical text as an infinite wellspring of meaning, attending to the minutest details and subtlest lexical connections between texts.

Freud's third definition of psychoanalysis is as a growing body of active scientific research, including case studies, research data on the mind and brain, and interpretations of other aspects and works of culture. Indeed, Freud did not restrict himself to analyzing individual human subjects, nor did he ignore other fields of academic research in the natural sciences and humanities. In fact, he was a prolific interpreter of culture, approaching it through scholarship in archeology, anthropology, linguistics, and literature.

Freud was particularly interested in religion. In addition to the many articles pertaining to the personal and social functions of religion, he wrote three major books on the subject. The first, *Totem and Taboo* (first published in German in 1913) develops a theory of religion based on a reconstruction of the psychological origins of primitive society. Following other religionists of his time, Freud notes two prohibitions, or taboos, common among most tribal cultures: incest and eating the tribe's totem animal. Unlike others, however, Freud insists that these actions would not have been prohibited unless there had also been the desire to do them. Freud sees both prohibitions as manifestations of the Oedipal Complex. Behind these prohibitions, he hypothesizes, was a tribal scene in which the sons collectively murdered their father, the chief, in order to have his wives/their mothers. Then, wracked with guilt, they identified that same father with a totem figure that became the sacred symbol of the tribe. In this way, the original patricide was symbolically prohibited. The two taboos, therefore, are prohibitions against an original Oedipal sin carried out by the tribal horde: incestuous desire for the mother and patricide.

Freud continued his speculations on religion in *The Future of an Illusion* (1927). Whereas *Totem and Taboo* explores the prehistoric past of human civilization, *The Future of an Illusion* focuses on present-day religion—more precisely, belief in God—and offers a projection concerning its future in modern society. If an **illusion** is something that one very much wishes to be true, then belief in God is, for Freud, an illusion. The reality of life in this world is brutal and final, and we humans seek something to help us cope with that reality. As children, we had parents to protect us from that reality and, above all, to help us believe that everything will be okay, that we are safe amid the storm. (Of course, the parent knows that such assurances are ultimately illusory.) As adults, we still need that kind of assurance in the illusion of safety and security, but we no longer have our parents to provide it. And that is the function of religion. It is a projection of what we want to be true, of a God who is the ultimate, ideal parent. Thus religion is an expression of wish fulfillment. The secret of the strength of religion, Freud contends, "lies in the strength of those wishes" (*The Future of an Illusion,* p.30). In this respect, Freud speculates, society's belief in God is something like a collective neurosis arising from the Oedipus Complex. As human society continues to evolve, to mature, thereby outgrowing childhood wishes and desires, Freud believes it will outgrow its need for such a father figure. Modern reason will replace illusion.

Freud's best known if also most imaginative work on religion is *Moses and Monotheism* (written between 1934 and 1938), in which he reconstructs the origins of ancient Israelite religion through a reading of the exodus story in the Hebrew Bible. As one might expect, Freud does not take the biblical account of Moses and the exodus at face value, but rather attempts to discover within it traces of a nearly forgotten story of the true origins of Israelite religion. Moses, he argues, was not originally Hebrew. He was an Egyptian prince who followed the teaching of Pharaoh Akhenaton, a religious revolutionary who wanted to replace the polytheism of Egypt with devotion to one god, Aten, a god of love and moral goodness. Akhenaton died and his monotheism lost favor in Egypt. His disciple Moses adopted the Hebrew slaves as his people and fled to the wilderness. In time, however, the Hebrews became disillusioned with Moses and his monotheism. They killed him, took their former tribal war god Yahweh as their deity, and renamed the high priest of that god Moses. The complex law codes and rituals of sacrifice in the Torah, Freud argues, are the legal remnants of this period in Israel's religious history. Centuries later, prophets such as Amos and Isaiah arose, rejecting the bloody rituals of that priestly god and calling for a return to the one god of love and morality advocated by the original, the Egyptian Moses. Their reforms led to the emergence of the higher moral religions of Jewish and Christian monotheism.

Needless to say, few historians of ancient Israelite religion have found Freud's imaginative reconstruction of the origins of Jewish monotheism compelling. However, despite his conclusions, his interpretive approach to this literature does provide an interesting way of looking at the religions of Judaism and Christianity as represented in their canons of scriptures. By reading biblical literature as a manifestation of conflict over time between two very different forms of religious belief and practice, Freud draws attention to it as a site of conflict and ambivalence, which, like the dreams and verbal slips of his patients, reveals far more than it consciously intends.

Further Reading

By Freud

The Interpretation of Dreams. First Part. In *The Standard Edition*. IV. London: Hogarth Press, 1953–74.

Obsessive Actions and Religious Practices. In *The Standard Edition*, IX. London: Hogarth Press, 1953–74.

Totem and Taboo: Some Points of Agreement between the Mental Lives of Savages and Neurotics. In *The Standard Edition*. XIII. London: Hogarth Press, 1953–74.

Introductory Lectures on Psycho-Analysis. In *The Standard Edition*. XV–XVI. London: Hogarth Press, 1953–74.

"The Uncanny." In *The Standard Edition*. XVII. London: Hogarth Press, 1953–74.

*"Two Encyclopedia Articles." In *The Standard Edition*, edited and translated by James Strachey in collaboration with Anna Freud. XVIII. London: Hogarth Press, 1953–74.

*The Future of an Illusion. In The Standard Edition. XXI. London: Hogarth Press, 1953–74.

Moses and Monotheism: Three Essays. In The Standard Edition. XXIII. London: Hogarth Press, 1953–74.

About Freud

Boyarin, Daniel. "An Imaginary and Desirable Converse: Moses and Monotheism as Family Romance." In Reading Bibles, Writing Bodies: Identity and The Book, edited by Timothy K. Beal and David M. Gunn. London and New York: Routledge, 1996.

Capps, Donald, ed. Freud and Freudians on Religion: A Reader. New Haven: Yale University Press, 2001.

Dicenso, James. The Other Freud: Religion, Culture, and Psychoanalysis. New York: Routledge, 1998.

*Gay, Peter. Freud: A Life for Our Times. New York: W.W. Norton, 1988.

Handelman, Susan A. The Slayers of Moses: The Emergence of Rabbinic Interpretation in Modern Literary Theory. Albany: State University of New York Press, 1982.

*Pals, Daniel. "Religion and Personality: Sigmund Freud." In Seven Theories of Religion. New York: Oxford University Press, 1996.

Rashkow, Ilona N. Taboo or Not Taboo: Sexuality and Family in the Hebrew Bible. Philadelphia: Fortress Press, 2000.

Ricoeur, Paul. Freud and Philosophy: An Essay on Interpretation. Translated by Denis Savage. New Haven: Yale University Press, 1970.

KARL MARX

Key Concepts

- historical materialism
- dialectic
- mode of production (relations and forces)
- proletariats, capitalists, bourgeoisie
- means of production
- base/superstructure
- alienation
- ideology

Karl Marx (1818–83) was a German political philosopher. He was born in Trier, Germany, to liberal Jewish parents who had become Protestant (Evangelical Established Church) in order to advance the law career of his father. In 1836, after a year at the University of Bonn, he entered the University of Berlin, where he concentrated on philosophy. Deeply influenced by Hegelian thought, he was a member of a student group known as the Young Hegelians who espoused a radical, atheistic version of Hegel's dialectic.

Marx's doctoral thesis on Greek philosophy was accepted in 1841. Unable to find a university position, he became a journalist for the liberal newspaper the *Rhenish Gazette*. He wrote articles on a wide range of topics, touching especially on political and social concerns, and served briefly as the paper's editor before it was censored by the Prussian government for, among other things, articles about worker conditions.

In 1843 Marx, newly married, moved to Paris to take a position as co-editor of a new publication, the *German-French Annals*. This journal expressed communist ideas and failed to draw the interest of the French. Deemed subversive by the Prussian government, the publication was confiscated and its editors sought for arrest. Once again unemployed, and now unable to return to Germany, Marx devoted his energy to writing a work of political philosophy that would express his socialist views. At this time (1844), Marx befriended Friedrich Engels

(1820–95), socialist son of a German industrialist, who became Marx's life-long collaborator and benefactor.

At the insistence of the Prussian government, the French expelled Marx and other German communists from Paris. Marx moved to Brussels, supported financially by Engels. In 1847 Marx and Engels attended the Congress of the Communist League in London, where Marx asserted his views on how to bring about a communist revolution. As a result, he and Engels were commissioned to articulate the league's working doctrines. This commission led to the publication of *The Communist Manifesto* (published in German in 1848).

After the 1848 French revolution, Marx moved first to Paris, then to Cologne, then back to Paris as conservative factions regained control of Germany, and then, late in the summer of 1849, to London, where he remained throughout the rest of his life. Marx lived in poverty for a time, but with Engels's support and his own family inheritances, he eventually enjoyed a comfortable lifestyle in London with his family. He continued to organize social movements and to write. In 1852, and continuing for ten years, he became a regular contributor to the *New York Tribune*. Marx published the first volume of *Das Kapital (Capital)*, a critique of capitalist economics, in German in 1867. *Das Kapital* brought attention to Marx's ideas and a second edition was published in 1871. Translations into other languages soon followed, though an English translation did not appear until after Marx's death. Two subsequent volumes of *Das Kapital* remained unfinished at Marx's death and were completed later by Engels.

Marxism, or Marxist theory, is based on ideas formulated by Marx and Engels as a critique of industrial capitalism. It focuses attention on social history in relation to political economy, especially class struggle. From a Marxist perspective, history is not driven by ideas, values, or some over-arching spirit. Rather, it is a record of struggle, rooted in material existence, for food, shelter, products of labor, and control over the means of production. Marx's ideas—disseminated, in part, through various interpretations of and elaborations on Marxism—had a tremendous impact on twentieth-century politics as well as on critical theory, literary theory, cultural studies, history, sociology, economics, the arts, philosophy, and religion.

We can conceive of Marxist theory in at least two ways. First, Marxist theory is a revolutionary critique of capitalist society. Marx was personally concerned with the need for social change in light of what he saw as the injustice and oppression caused by nineteenth-century industrial capitalism and the economic relations it engendered. His analysis of how industrial capitalism operated and caused oppression was directed at changing this system, thereby ending the human suffering that it produced. Second, and more important for our purposes, Marxist theory is a way to analyze not only economic relations, but also those values and viewpoints created by industrial capitalism that impact ostensibly nonpolitical endeavors such as religion, literature, and other cultural products and practices. Marxist theory underscores the ideological nature of all human enterprises.

Central to Marxist thought is Marx's philosophy of history. Known as **historical materialism**, it views historical change as the result of the actions of human beings within the material world, and not as the hand of God or some other extrahuman or spiritual force. In this materialist view of history, Marx was influenced by Ludwig Feuerbach (1804–72), who emphasized the material conditions of the world and was critical of the idealism of Hegelian thinking, which stressed ideas and the spiritual nature of the universe and historical change. For Marx, what propels history is a **dialectic** expressing economic and other conflicts between social classes. Hegel, too, had understood history as dialectical, with change taking place as a series of successive movements from thesis to antithesis to synthesis. Whereas Hegel saw this as a history of the human spirit, Marx saw it as a history of human struggle over material goods and their production. This is why Marx is said to have stood Hegel on his head. Material circumstances shape ideas, not vice versa.

Marxism describes the historical development of different **modes of production**, a concept referring to the ways societies organize economic relations in order to allow for the production of goods. The Marxist characterization of capitalism as an oppressive and unjust system of labor and production centers on social relations and the tools used in the production of goods. Labor is not performed in isolation, but within larger human networks. Human patterns of economic organization, or **relations of production**, interact with human labor and technologies, or **forces of production**, to create the mode of production.

Modes of production differ across historical periods. Marxist cultural analysis is especially focused on industrial capitalism, viewing it as an economic system that promotes an unequal, and therefore unjust, mode of production. Marx's discussion of class struggle in capitalist society predicates that economic development progresses from primitive to feudal to capitalist, and that class struggle corresponds to the dominant mode of production in each society. It is only with the development of a socialist mode of production that class distinctions and conflicts end. Historical change can occur only within the context of dialectical conflicts between classes. Contradictions between those in control and those controlled inevitably lead to class conflict. It is the dialectic of class confrontations that engenders a new society. The ultimate goal, of course, is a socialist, classless state.

In a capitalist mode of production, the relations of production are such that workers labor to turn raw material into finished goods, and owners control the sale and distribution of these products, collecting their surplus value. Such a system, says Marx, inevitably results in creation of class distinctions in which the **proletariat**—workers who sell their labor power for a wage in order to make a living—enables the **capitalists** who own and control the **means of**

production (that is, the natural resources, factories, machines, and other material resources) to recover a profit at the expense of the workers. A third class, the **bourgeoisie**, are neither owners nor workers, but service providers such as teachers and doctors. Although they provide services to both other classes, they are usually identified as having the same class as capitalists.

For Marx, economic organization (that is, modes of production) shapes other aspects of society. The concepts of **base and superstructure** explain this relationship. Base refers to a society's economic mode of production, which determines its superstructure, that is, its political, social, religious, artistic, moral, scientific, and other cultural productions. From this perspective, religion, for instance, is not an independent or autonomous mode of human activity, but is conditioned and determined by a society's mode of production and the relations of production it engenders. Superstructure, then, is a materialist theory, viewing religion as part of a society's superstructure.

The economic base is supported by a superstructure that justifies the base and seeks to naturalize class differences as an overarching reality that people have no possibility of changing. Such a system is understood by Marxism as fundamentally exploitative and only changeable through the dialectical struggle between classes. Struggle occurs because the inequities and contradictions of an unequal system become evident over time. Marxism forecasts that the dialectical struggle will eventually destroy capitalism and establish a class-free socialism in its place. This event will mark the end of history in the sense that further economic change will no longer occur because unequal class relations that fueled the dialectical struggle have ceased to exist.

Marxism draws attention to processes of **alienation**, especially through the stratification of society into different social classes, in which the upper classes have privileged access to the goods produced by the lower classes. Alienation— a result of unequal class relations caused by a capitalist mode of production— occurs in two ways. First, a capitalist mode of production is a system in which workers produce goods from which only capitalist owners profit. This is labor alienated from its own efforts. Second, workers are alienated from themselves in a capitalist system. According to Marx, this occurs because workers become commodities when they must sell their alienated labor in the marketplace, just as other goods are sold. Thus, workers are alienated from their own humanity.

Marxist theory conceives of **ideology** as a false consciousness that distorts social and material reality, functioning to keep people in their place within the capitalist system. This distortion prevents people from viewing relations of production as they really are. Therefore, ideology is an aspect of superstructure: it is produced by the economic base and functions to legitimate that base. Ideologies determine what can be thought and believed about politics, religion, literature, and other aspects of culture. But ideologies are not autonomous; they depend, says Marx, on the prevailing economic mode of production and serve as a justification for its continued existence. The Protestant work ethic, for instance, promoted the value of hard work and profit making without desire for personal gain. This way of working was understood to be the will of God. Thus profit seeking was equated with religious duty. From a Marxist perspective, the Protestant work ethic exemplifies an ideology that legitimates an economic mode of production that requires workers to toil long hours under difficult working conditions. The laborer who espouses this work ethic falsely understands his or her hard work as freely choosing to follow the will of God, but such a view is in fact a distortion of reality, promoting a mode of production that oppresses workers in order to benefit capitalist owners. One labors under the illusion of choice or free will when in fact there is none.

Marx's most famous assertion of the ideological nature of religion is found in his description of religion as "the opium of the people." This phrase refers to the Marxist claim that religion promises future reward and justice in the afterlife in order to render tolerable those injustices and oppressions experienced in this life. Religion's deferral of justice to the afterlife keeps the oppressed masses from rebelling against the ruling classes who exploit their labor. From a Marxist view, then, religion can be adequately understood only when it takes into account how texts, rituals, and other religious phenomena are implicated in a culture's material conditions, especially the dominant economic modes of production.

Further Reading

By Marx

*Marx, Karl, and Friedrich Engels. *On Religion*. Classics in Religious Studies 3. Chico, CA: Scholars Press and The American Academy of Religion, 1982.

Elster, Jon, ed., *Karl Marx: A Reader*. Cambridge: Cambridge University Press, 1986.

Karl Marx: Selected Writings. Edited by David McLellan. 2nd ed. Oxford: Oxford University Press, 2000.

The Marx-Engels Reader. Edited By Robert C. Tucker. 2nd ed. New York: W. W. Norton and Company, 1978.

About Marx

Carver, Terrell, ed. *The Cambridge Companion to Marx*. Cambridge: Cambridge University Press, 1992.

Elster, Jon. *Making Sense of Marx*. Cambridge: Cambridge University Press, 1985.

*McLellan, David. *Karl Marx: His Life and Thought*. New York: Harper and Row, 1973.

McLellan, David. *Marxism and Religion: A Description and Assessment of the Marxist Critique of Christianity*. New York: Harper and Row, 1987.

*Pals, Daniel L. "Religion as Alienation: Karl Marx." In *Seven Theories of Religion*. New York: Oxford University Press, 1996.

Phillips, D. Z., ed. *Can Religion Be Explained Away?* New York: St. Martin's Press, 1996.

Singer, Peter. *Marx: A Very Short Introduction*. Oxford: Oxford University Press, 2000.

Turner, Denys. "Religion: Illusions and Liberation." In *The Cambridge Companion to Marx*, edited by Terrell Carver. Cambridge: Cambridge University Press, 1992.

Wolff, Jonathan. *Why Read Marx Today?* Oxford and New York: Oxford University Press, 2002.

FRIEDRICH NIETZSCHE

Key Concepts

- Dionysian and Apollonian
- power
- good, bad, and evil
- slave morality
- death of God
- overman

Friedrich Wilhelm Nietzsche (1844–1900) was born in Röcken, Prussia. He was the eldest of three children. His father and both grandfathers were ordained ministers in the Lutheran Church, and early on he seemed destined for the ministry (other children called him "little pastor"). His father died at thirty-six when Friedrich was only five. About five months later his baby brother, Joseph, also died and was buried wrapped in his father's arms.

Nietzsche received an excellent education. From fourteen to nineteen he studied at Schulpforta, an elite boarding school. In 1864 he entered the University of Bonn to study theology and philology, but a year later moved to the University of Leipzig to focus exclusively on philology. In 1867 he took leave of his studies to serve for a year in the Prussian military as an officer in the horse-drawn artillery. In 1869, at twenty-four, he was appointed professor of classical philology at the University of Basel. At the time of his appointment he had yet to complete his exams and dissertation, but the University of Leipzig waived those requirements and awarded him the doctoral degree. In 1870 he took leave from the university to serve as a medic in the Franco-Prussian war, but was discharged within months due to a serious illness.

As a result of failing health, Nietzsche took leave of his professorate in 1876, and then resigned in 1879. Having given up his Prussian citizenship without being granted Swiss citizenship, he remained "stateless" for the rest of his life. For the next ten years, he wrote prolifically while traveling and visiting friends throughout Europe and elsewhere.

In January 1889, while in Turin, he suffered a mental breakdown from which he never recovered. The story goes that he collapsed after wrapping his arms around the neck of a horse that had just been brutally whipped by a coachman. After a year in a sanitarium in Jena, he lived with his mother until her death in 1897, and then spent his last years with his sister Elizabeth, a devout anti-Semite who published *The Will To Power* (based on his 1880s notebooks) and who later brought Nietzsche's works to the attention of influential Nazis, including Hitler and Mussolini. In fact, although there are certain passages in his writings that easily support the anti-Jewish ideology of the Nazis, Nietzsche hated German nationalism and expressed much alienation from his sister on account of her anti-Semitism.

Nietzsche described his work as philosophizing "with a hammer." Trained in classical philology, he is best known as a critic of prevailing western European cultural values. In particular, he challenged the Christian foundations of those values. His philosophy was not simply negative or destructive, as some unfairly represent it. On the contrary, his critical eye on Western civilization was inspired by the desire to affirm what he understood to be the source of life—a kind of primordial, creative energy beyond rationality and beyond moral categorization as good or evil. He believed that Western civilization was in decline because it had drained that life force, ceding power and authority to those who fear it.

Nietzsche's first book, *The Birth of Tragedy* (published in German in 1872) describes this creative, primordial life force as **Dionysian**, after the ancient gender-bending god of wine, masquerade, violence, and orgy. Contrary to the prevailing view of ancient Greece as a world of noble harmony and rational order, Nietzsche argued that Greek culture existed in the tension between two opposing forces: on the one hand, the **Apollonian** forces of moral order and sober rationality; on the other hand, the Dionysian forces of amoral desire and nonrational, creative exuberance. The Apollonian is order; the Dionysian is primordial, that is, the chaotic life force that precedes the order of civilization and is its creative source. Nietzsche believed that in the centuries since ancient Greece, Western civilization had gradually repressed the Dionysian, leaving modern Western society predominantly Apollonian, starved of creative energy and in poor health. Therefore, he called for a resurrection of the Dionysian and looked to the German music and art of his time as a potential savior.

Already in *The Birth of Tragedy* we see Nietzsche's conception of the world as a turbulent sea of nonrational forces that are both destructive and generative. Contrary to the predominant Christian worldview of his time, Nietzsche saw the world not as a moral universe, created and managed by a moral God, but as a chaotic "monster of energy" in which humans live and move and have their being. **Power**, therefore, must be understood not as an object to be held but as a never-ending struggle within this ever-changing sea of forces. Life, therefore, is driven by a will to power that is antecedent to morality.

Of particular importance to twentieth-century thought about religion is Nietzsche's *On the Genealogy of Morals* (1887), which explores the origins of contemporary moral categories of **good, bad**, and **evil**. He argues that these categories are not essential or universal categories but are culturally constructed through operations of social power through history. Goodness is simply that which is valued by those in power, and badness is its opposite, either as a threat to their power (e.g., enemies) or as the antithesis of it (e.g., the weak). In the earliest stages of human history, Nietzsche argues, the good and the bad were determined by the dominant knightly-aristocratic class. That which furthered their health and happiness in the world was good; that which did not was bad. Then came moralistic religion, the champions of which Nietzsche calls the priestly-aristocratic class. Whereas the knightly-aristocratic values were based on this-worldly physical pleasure and the furtherance of life, the priestly-aristocratic values were just the opposite, glorifying selflessness and weakness and calling the knightly-aristocratic affirmation of life and health not just bad but downright "evil." (Like other late nineteenth-century German historians, he identifies this priestly-aristocratic class quite explicitly with Roman Catholic and Jewish priesthoods and legal codes.) Against them, the priestly-aristocratic class has established a **slave morality** that glorifies weakness and makes people feel bad for all that comes naturally, that is, for their will to power, pleasure, and the enjoyment of life.

Historians and anthropologists would rightly doubt Nietzsche's provocative, if also simplistic, history of society as he presents it in *Genealogy*. The importance of this work for religious studies, however, lies not in his account of the origins of religion in relation to this historical schema but in his genealogical approach. Instead of seeing religious ideas and values like "evil" as universal truths or divine revelations, he approaches them as products of history that take form over time through ongoing social struggle. They are, in short, effects of power.

The first thing that comes to most minds concerning Nietzsche and religion is, of course, his pronouncement of the **death of God** in *The Gay Science* (1882; section 125) and the Prologue to *Thus Spoke Zarathustra* (1883–85). It is important to understand Nietzsche's meaning here. He is not calling for or celebrating the death of God, but is describing what he sees as a fact of modern Western civilization, namely that it no longer lives by faith in "God" as a monolithic, ultimate author and guarantor of moral law who sees into the hearts of all people and will judge them accordingly. For Nietzsche, the most important thing about the death of God is what must die with him, namely, the Christian conceptions of human sinfulness, fallenness, and indebtedness. Nietzsche's interest in making this pronouncement is to free people from bondage to a slave morality according to which life is lived in hopes of some future, other-worldly reward. We see this most clearly, perhaps, in his Prologue of *Thus Spoke Zarathustra*. Zarathustra, the hero of exuberant freedom and affirmation of life on earth, meets a saint in the forest. Whereas Zarathustra loves the earth and human beings, the saint has given up on humans and seeks only to love God. As the saint departs, Zarathustra wonders to himself, "Could it be possible? This old saint in the forest has not yet heard anything of this, that *God is dead*!" (p. 12). Immediately following this interchange with the old saint, Zarathustra begins preaching the coming of the **overman** (*Übermensch*, often translated "superman"), that is, the human being who has overcome the Christian notion of human nature as fallen and sinful and the slave morality that goes with it.

Further Reading
By Nietzsche

The Birth of Tragedy and The Case of Wagner. Translated By Walter Kaufmann. New York: Random House, 1967.

Beyond Good and Evil. Translated By Walter Kaufmann. New York: Random House, 1966.

**On the Genealogy of Morals* and *Ecce Homo*. Translated by Walter Kaufmann and R. J. Hollingdale. New York: Random House, 1967.

The Gay Science, with a Prelude of Rhymes and an Appendix of Songs. Translated by Walter Kaufmann. New York: Random House, 1974.

Daybreak: Thoughts on the Prejudices of Morality. Translated by R. J. Hollingdale. Cambridge: Cambridge University Press, 1982.

The Will to Power. Translated by Walter Kaufmann. New York: Random House, 1967.

**Thus Spoke Zarathustra*. Translated by Walter Kaufmann. New York: Viking, 1968.

About Nietzsche

Bataille, Georges. *On Nietzsche*. Translated by Bruce Boone. London: Athlone Press, 1992.

Friedman, Richard Elliot. "Nietzsche at Turin." In *The Hidden Face of God*. San Francisco: HarperSanFrancisco, 1995.

Kaufmann, Walter. *Nietzsche: Philosopher, Psychologist, Antichrist*. Princeton: Princeton University Press, 1950.

Mandel, Siegfried. *Nietzsche and the Jews*. New York: Prometheus Books, 1998.

Murphy, Tim. *Nietzsche, Metaphor, Religion*. Albany: State University of New York Press, 2001.

*Nehamas, Alexander. *Nietzsche: Life as Literature*. Cambridge, Mass.: Harvard University Press, 1985.

FERDINAND DE SAUSSURE

Key Concepts

- structural linguistics/structuralism
- semiology/semiotics
- langue/parole
- synchronic/diachronic
- sign (signifier and signified)
- arbitrariness of the sign
- binary opposition (meaning as difference)

Ferdinand de Saussure (1857–1913) was a Swiss linguist whose posthumously published *Course in General Linguistics* (1916) became a catalyst for the development of structuralism. Saussure was born in Geneva, Switzerland, into a family with a lineage of noted academics going back to the eighteenth century. Saussure himself displayed a gift for languages from an early age. At the University of Geneva, he studied not only linguistics but also theology, law, and chemistry. In 1878, at twenty-one years old, he published *Memoir on the Original System of Vowels in the Indo-European Languages*, a comparative study of vowel usage in proto-Indo-European languages.

Saussure received his doctorate from the University of Leipzig in 1880. From 1881 to 1891 he taught linguistics at the École des Hautes Études in Paris. In 1891 he returned to the University of Geneva, where he taught courses on Sanskrit and general linguistics for the remainder of his career. Although he published very little, his students at the University of Geneva, compiled and transcribed their notes from his general linguistics course lectures and had them published in 1916 under the title *Course in General Linguistics*.

As detailed in *Course in General Linguistics*, Saussure's perspective on language has impacted many fields of academic inquiry including religion, literature, philosophy, anthropology, and psychology. In the work of influential twentieth-century critical theorists—such as Michel **FOUCAULT**, Louis **ALTHUSSER**, Roland **BARTHES**, Claude Lévi-Strauss, Jacques **LACAN**, Julia **KRISTEVA**, and

Jacques **DERRIDA**—Saussure's assertion that linguistic meaning resides in the relationships between words has constituted a critical point of departure. Saussure's philosophy of language is commonly referred to as **structural linguistics** since its strategy for examining language and meaning centers on investigating structures within a system. In concert with the work of Martin Heidegger and other philosophers of being, **structuralism** brought about a major shift in twentieth-century thought, often referred to as the "linguistic turn," which has become shorthand for the conviction that meaning does not exist outside language.

In *Course in General Linguistics*, Saussure advocates the scientific study of language, which, for him, concerns "the life of signs within society." This method contrasts with historical linguistics as then practiced by European philologists who sought to trace Indo-European languages back to a common origin. Saussure called his new linguistic science **"semiology,"** a term derived from the Greek word for "sign" (*semeîon*). Semiology, also called **semiotics**, is the science of signs, that is, the study of the structure of language as a system of signification rather than the history of language.

In order to study language as a system of signs, Saussure makes a distinction between **langue** and **parole**. *Langue* ("language") refers to language as a structured system operating at a particular time and place, and to the linguistic rules that determine how a language can be used in practice. In contrast, *parole* ("speech") refers to particular instances of speech within the system. Without *langue*, *parole*—what individuals say—would be impossible. For Saussure, the object of inquiry, then, is langue, which constitutes an overarching linguistic system that makes specific utterances possible.

As the terms *langue* and *parole* suggest, the study of language as a system requires a **synchronic** ("at the same time") rather than a **diachronic** ("through time") approach. Synchrony refers to the study of language—especially spoken language—as it is used at a particular moment in time. Diachrony refers to the study of language over time. Nineteenth-century philology employed a diachronic methodology that derived from a central assumption that language could only be comprehended through a study of its historical changes. Thus, if a word could be traced back to its origin, then the path to its present meaning could be followed.

Saussure advocates a synchronic approach to language as a system, asserting that language can only be understood in terms of relationship. Instead of etymology as the conveyor of a word's meaning, Saussure argues that meaning is produced by a word's relationship to other words occurring at a particular time, within a particular system of relationships. Thus, for instance, the contemporary word "dog" means something not because of its historical derivation from the Middle English *dogge,* which is in turn derived from the Old English *docga*, but rather because of the current relationship of "dog" to other words like "puppy" and "cat." In Saussure's analysis, all of these terms are part of a system, and their meanings and significances derive from relationships with other signs within that system.

As illustrated by the previous example, a central claim made by Saussure's synchronic linguistic analysis is that words do not have inherent meaning. Instead, meaning resides in relationships of difference and similarity within a larger linguistic system—words are not units of self-contained meaning. A related concern—whether language is natural or conventional—also plays an important role in Saussure's linguistic analysis. A natural view of language proposes that language names things in the world because there is some intrinsic relationship between a word and the thing named. By contrast, if language is conventional, both concrete things and abstract concepts are named on the basis of an arbitrary decision to use a certain sound to represent a certain idea. As we will see, Saussure develops a theory of language that clearly sides with the idea of language as conventional.

How does Saussure arrive at the conclusion that language is primarily conventional? He starts with the idea of the linguistic **sign**. A sign may be a word or some other form. Regardless of its particular form, however, every sign consists of a **signifier** and a **signified**.

$$sign = \frac{signifier}{signified}$$

A linguistic sign comprises a sound-image, such as the letters d-o-g spoken or written (the signifier) and the object or concept associated with the sound-image (the signified). What determines the signification (i.e., meaning) of a sign is not its sound-image or linguistic origin, but its place within the larger network of interrelationships, that is, within the larger linguistic structure. Thus a structuralist approach focuses on the relationship of individual parts to the larger whole—the structure—within which significance is determined.

One of Saussure's key insights, then, is that the sign is fundamentally relational. Further, the relationship between the signifier and the signified is **arbitrary**. That is, any signifier can potentially stand for any signified. The fact that *dog* signifies a four-legged domestic animal in English, while *chien* and *inu* point to this same animal in French and Japanese respectively, is evidence that there is no necessary relationship between the letters d-o-g and a common pet. The word *dog* is an arbitrary designation. We could call dogs by some other term as long as we agree culturally on that usage. There is no particular dog designated by the word, nor is there some inherent quality ("dogness") contained in or conveyed by the sound-image *dog*.

Since signs are arbitrary, the meaning of any particular sign is determined in terms of similarity and difference in relation to other signs. Thus meaning is founded on **binary oppositions**, such as light/dark, good/bad, inside/outside, margin/center, male/female, positive/negative, immanent/transcendent, life/death, sacred/profane, and so on. Within these binary pairs, the meaning of one is basically the opposite of the other. Meaning, then, is predicated on difference. Sacred means "not profane," inside means "not outside," and so on. Saussure argues:

> In language there are only differences. Even more important: a difference generally implies positive terms between which the difference is set up; but in language there are only differences *without positive terms*. Whether we take the signified or the signifier, language has neither ideas nor sounds that existed before the linguistic system, but only conceptual and phonic differences that have issued from the system. The idea or phonic substance that a sign contains is of less importance than the other signs that surround it. (Baskin, trans., *Course in General Linguistics,* p. 120)

Saussure's insights into the structure of language have significant implications for the academic study of religion. For instance, religious narratives frequently derive meaning from binary oppositions. Western monotheisms relate stories that pit good against evil. While some may assume that good and evil name real, material conditions in the world, Saussure's analysis of language forces us to ask whether good and evil exist prior to language or only within the binary relationships of terms in particular languages. If good and evil naturally name aspects of the external, objective world, how is it, we might ask, that some traditions understand the world in terms of binary oppositions other than good and evil? In Japan, for instance, good/evil as a binary opposition is far less important historically than the binary opposition of purity/impurity as a conceptual pair used to make ethical judgments. Similarly, the opposition of sacred/profane has had a profound influence on ways that the academic study of religion conceptualizes its subject matter. But do sacred/profane name an external reality or craft that reality arbitrarily through language?

Further Reading

By Saussure

Course in General Linguistics. Translated by Wade Baskin. New York and London: McGraw-Hill, 1959.

About Saussure

Belsey, Catherine. *Poststructuralism: A Very Short Introduction.* Oxford: Oxford University Press, 2002.

Culler, Jonathan. *The Pursuit of Signs: Semiotics, Literature, Deconstruction.* Ithaca, N.Y.: Cornell University Press, 1981.

*Culler, Jonathan. *Ferdinand de Saussure*. Rev. ed. Ithaca, N.Y.: Cornell University Press, 1986.

Jensen, Jeppe Sinding. "Structure." In *Guide to the Study of Religion*, edited by Willi Braun and Russell T. McCutcheon. London and New York: Cassell, 2000.

Lévi-Strauss, Claude. "The Structural Study of Myth." In *Structural Anthropology*. New York: Basic Books, 1963.

Murphy, Tim. "Speaking Different Languages: Religion and the Study of Religion." In *Secular Theories of Religion: Current Perspectives*, edited by Tim Jensen and Mikael Rothstein. Copenhagen: Museum Tusculanum Press, 2000.

THE THEORISTS

LOUIS ALTHUSSER

Key Concepts

- base and superstructure
- practices
- ideology
- Repressive State Apparatuses
- Ideological State Apparatuses
- interpellation

Louis Althusser (1918–90) was a French Marxist political philosopher. He was born in Algeria and educated in Algiers and France. He was admitted to the École normale supérieure in 1939, but World War II disrupted his studies when he was called to military duty. During the German occupation of France, Althusser was captured and placed in a German prison camp where he remained until the end of the war. Freed, he resumed his studies. In 1948 Althusser completed a master's thesis on the German philosopher Hegel and later passed the *agrégation* in philosophy and was given a teaching appointment.

Althusser was a practicing Catholic for the first thirty years of his life, and during that period displayed a strong interest in Catholic monastic life and traditions. In the late 1940s, Althusser joined the Communist Party and remained a member for the remainder of his life. During the May 1968 Paris strikes, he was in a sanitarium recuperating from a bout of depression, an illness he struggled with throughout his life. Unlike some of his contemporary intellectuals, he supported the Communist Party in denying the revolutionary nature of the student movement, though he later reversed this view.

Althusser murdered his wife in 1980. Declared incompetent to stand trial, he was institutionalized but released in 1983. He subsequently lived in near isolation in Paris and died in 1990 of a heart attack. During the last years of his life, he wrote two different versions of his autobiography, both of which were published posthumously in 1992 (both are included in the 1995 edition of *The Future Lasts Forever*).

Althusser is especially important for the ways in which he reinterpreted Marx's ideas and made them resonate with intellectual currents prevalent in the 1960s, including structuralist ideas. Althusser's work is sometimes referred to as "structuralist Marxism" or "postmodern Marxism." Regardless of labels, his rereading of Marx aimed at liberating Marxist ideas from their Soviet interpretation, as well as from humanistic interpretations. This rereading was meant to revitalize Marxist ideas and to put them back to use for revolutionary purposes.

Of Althusser's many writings, three have been particularly influential: *For Marx* (first published in French in 1965), *Reading Capital* (first published in French in 1968), and the oft-cited long essay "Ideology and Ideological State Apparatuses" (written in 1969; included in *"Lenin and Philosophy" and Other Essays*). Althusser's influence has been widespread, shaping such diverse fields as cultural studies, film studies, and Marxist literary theory.

Althusser's reassessment of Marxism included his rejection of some key Marxist assumptions about society. For instance, he argued against the version of determinism found in the classic Marxist formulation of **base and superstructure**. Base refers to the particular economic "mode of production" operating in a given society. Different societies are organized around different economic systems (modes of production)—for instance, agricultural, capitalist, or planned. The concept of superstructure refers to political, social, religious, and other noneconomic aspects of a society. Superstructure, then, includes the political and cultural aspects of a society, for instance, governmental, educational, religious, and other institutional structures. The traditional Marxist view was that base determines superstructure. That is, political, social, and religious spheres—the superstructure—are not autonomous but are dependent on and conditioned by the economic mode, or base. Althusser prefers to talk about the idea of social formation (that is, society) consisting of three practices: the economic, the political, and the ideological. Althusser sees base and superstructure in relationship and affords superstructure considerable autonomy, though in the end, he concedes, the economic is determinant even if it is not dominant in a particular historical moment.

The term **practices** has a specific meaning for Althusser, indicating processes of transformation: "By *practice* in general I shall mean any process of *transformation* of determinate given raw material into a determinate *product*, a transformation effected by a determinate human labour, using determinate means (of 'production')" (*For Marx*, p. 166). Economic practices are concerned with using human labor and other modes of production in order to transform raw materials (nature) into finished (social) products. Political practices deal with the uses of revolution to transform social relations, and ideological practices concern the uses of ideology to transform lived social relations, that is, the ways a subject relates to the lived conditions of existence. Theory is often treated as the opposite of practice, but for Althusser theory is a type of practice.

The term **ideology** is central to Althusser's theoretical agenda. In "Ideology and Ideological State Apparatuses," Althusser melds ideas taken from both Marxist and psychoanalytic thought in order to develop his theory of ideology and its relationship to subjectivity. Althusser's central concern in this essay is how a capitalist society reproduces existing modes of production and how they relate to people. Why do people support this process when, according to Marxist thought, they are in effect acceding to their own domination by the ruling classes? Althusser formulates his answer through the concepts of ideology, ideological state apparatuses, and interpollation (on which see below).

The reproduction of capitalist society occurs at two levels, the repressive and the ideological. On the one hand, social control can be coerced by the exertion of repressive force through such institutions as police, armies, courts, and prisons—what Althusser calls **Repressive State Apparatuses** (RSAs). These institutions suppress dissent and maintain the social order as envisioned by the ruling power. But application of repressive force is not the only way to guarantee assent to capitalism. In addition to RSAs, Althusser argues that ideology must also be employed to maintain the dominant social formation. Althusser refers to these ideological modes of control as **Ideological State Apparatuses** (ISAs)—including education, family, religion, sports, television, newspapers, and other media—which reproduce capitalist values, standards, and assumptions. Ideological discourse produced by ISAs acts on individual subjects in such a way that they see themselves and others as standing within the dominant ideology, subject to it, and willingly supportive—consciously or unconsciously—of the replication of this ruling power. In short, ideology imposes itself on us, but at the same time we act, in effect, as willing agents of the ideological agenda.

Departing from the earlier Marxist notion that ideology is false consciousness, Althusser understands ideology as an inevitable aspect of all societies—even socialist societies where capitalist exploitation has presumably been destroyed—that serves, in part, to provide human subjects with identities. For Althusser, "Ideology represents the imaginary relationship of individuals to their real conditions of existence" ("Ideology and Ideological State Apparatuses," p. 162). Distinguishing between the imaginary and the real allows Althusser to counter the traditional Marxist notion that ideologies are false because they mask an otherwise accessible and transparent real world. In contrast to this notion of ideology as misrepresentation, Althusser views ideology as a narrative or story we tell ourselves in order to understand our relationship to modes of production. A real, objective world is not accessible to us, only its representations are.

Ideology, then, is a discourse that has marked effects on each individual subject. Althusser understands this effect through the concept of **interpellation**.

Ideology hails and positions ("interpellates") individual subjects—or to state it another way, gives us a subject position—within particular discourses. As Althusser puts it, "ideology 'acts' or 'functions' in such a way that it . . . 'transforms' the individuals into subjects" ("Ideology and Ideological State Apparatuses," p. 174). We assume our interpellated position, identify with received social meanings, locate ourselves within these meanings, and enact its goals under the guise of having freedom to make this choice in the first place. Althusser's structuralist notion of ideology is antihumanist because it questions the centrality of the autonomous, freely choosing individual in this process. For Althusser, the subject is subjected to the ruling ideology, this mistaking ideological interpellation for the actions of a freely choosing individual.

Althusser provides an example of interpellation in action. Suppose, he says, an individual is hailed (interpellated) in the street by a policeman who says, "Hey, you there!" The individual turns around to face the policeman. Althusser states, "By this mere 180-degree physical conversion, he becomes a *subject*. Why? Because he has recognized that the hail was 'really' addressed to him, and that 'it was *really him* who was hailed' (and not someone else)" ("Ideology and Ideological State Apparatuses" 174). The hailing or interpellation of the individual creates a subject who is, without necessarily knowing it, acceding to the ideology of state authority, its laws, and the systems that support and generate it. Ideology transforms us into subjects that think and behave in socially acceptable ways.

Although ideology is understood to subject individuals to the needs and interests of the ruling classes, it is not, according to Althusser, fixed and unchangeable. Rather, ideology always contains contradictions and logical inconsistencies, which are discoverable. This means that the interpellated subject has at least some room to undo or destabilize the ideological process. Change or revolution is possible.

Althusser's work has numerous implications for religious studies. In particular, it draws our attention to the ways specific religious discourses (liturgies and other rituals, preaching, scriptures) function to interpellate or "recruit" its subjects into a particular ideological framework. Consider, for example, Carol A. Newsom's study of the first nine chapters of the Book of Proverbs ("Woman and the Discourse of Patriarchal Wisdom"). Newsom shows how this discourse—presented as a father speaking to a son—constructs a patriarchal ideology and locates the two of them within it, framed by the good domestic woman on the one hand and the dangerously attractive woman on the other. Newsom's study is an excellent model for how the religion scholar might use Althusser's concepts to analyze the power of a religious discourse (an ISA) to construct an individual's subjectivity according to a larger ideological structure.

Further Reading

By Althusser

For Marx. Translated by Ben Brewster. New York: Pantheon, 1969.

*"Ideology and Ideological State Apparatuses." In *"Lenin and Philosophy" and Other Essays*, translated by Ben Brewster. London: New Left Books, 1971.

(with Étienne Balibar) *Reading Capital.* Translated by Ben Brewster. London: New Left Books, 1977.

The Future Lasts Forever: A Memoir. Translated by Olivier Corpet, Yann Moulier Boutang, and Richard Veasey. New York: The New Press, 1995.

About Althusser

Kaplan, E. Ann, and Michael Sprinkler, eds. *The Althusserian Legacy.* London, Verso, 1993.

*Montag, Warren. *Louis Althusser.* New York: Palgrave, 2003.

Newsom, Carol A. "Woman and the Discourse of Patriarchal Wisdom: A Study of Proverbs 1–9." In *Gender and Difference in Ancient Israel*, edited by Peggy L. Day. Minneapolis: Fortress Press, 1989.

Payne, Michael. *Reading Knowledge: An Introduction to Barthes, Foucault, and Althusser.* Oxford: Blackwell, 1997.

Smith, Steven B. *Reading Althusser: An Essay on Structural Marxism.* Ithaca, N.Y.: Cornell University Press, 1984.

Valantasis, Richard. "Constructions of Power in Asceticism." *Journal of the American Academy of Religion* 63 (1995): 775–821.

MIKHAIL BAKHTIN

Key Concepts

- theoretism
- everyday life
- unfinalizabilty
- dialogism
- dialogic truth
- carnival

Mikhail Mikhailovich Bakhtin (1895–1975) was a radical theorist of literature and language. Influenced by the writings of Karl **MARX**, he was particularly interested in social transformation and revolution within dominant social and intellectual structures. Born in Orel, Russia, he was educated in philology and classics at the University of Petrograd (1914–18) during World War I and the Russian Revolution. He taught in Nevel and then Vitebsk, where he married Elena Aleksandrovna and became part of an intellectual circle that also included Valentin Voloshinov and Pavel Medvedev. He moved to Leningrad in 1924 and five years later was arrested for alleged participation in the underground Russian Orthodox Church. On account of ill health due to a bone disease, his initial sentence of ten years in a Siberian labor camp was reduced to six years of internal exile in Kazakhstan, where he worked as bookkeeper on a collective farm. After his exile, he had no long-term stable employment until 1945, when he began teaching Russian and world literature at Mordovia Pedagogical Institute in Saransk, where he remained until his retirement in 1961. Indeed, his academic life was so obscure that when scholars became interested in his work in the 1950s (based mainly on *Problems of Dostoevsky's Poetics*, originally published in Russian in 1929), many were surprised to find that he was still alive. In 1969 he moved to Moscow, where he remained until his death in 1975.

In Western Europe, initial interest in Bakhtin's work is owed primarily to Julia **KRISTEVA**'s famous 1969 essay, "Word, Dialogue, and Novel," in which she engages his theory of dialogism (see below) in order to develop her theory of intertextuality. Kristeva also wrote the introduction to the French translation of *Problems of Dostoevsky's Poetics*, published in 1970.

Bakhtin worked on many topics over a half century of writing, from ethics to aesthetics. In all his work, however, there is a general concern with the relationship between ethical responsibility and creativity. Put another way, he was interested in the relation between system and change, fixation and flux, law and revolution. How is change, as creative transformation of what is established and taken for granted, possible? What are the tensions within society, and within the self, between the desire for normativity and stability on the one hand and innovation and openness on the other? What is one's ethical responsibility to maintain and support established social order on the one hand and to bring about social transformation on the other?

From his earliest writings, he attacked "**theoretism,**" that is, the reduction of human creativity to a theoretical system. Theoretism impoverishes the truth of human life by subordinating all the complexity and messiness of human subjectivity and social relations to a static intellectual system.

Resisting theoretism, Bakhtin attended to the particularities of everyday life. Such attention to the minutiae of the everyday undermines the scholarly impulse toward universal theories. By the same token, he was drawn not to the grand or catastrophic events of human history—wars, disasters, revolutions, inaugurations—but **everyday life**, the "prosaic" details of the lives of ordinary people, details that are in many ways most revealing of human society and how social transformation takes place in history.

Throughout his work, Bakhtin emphasized "**unfinalizability,**" that is, the impossibility of any final conclusion. Nothing in life has been finalized, and nothing in life can ever be finalized. As he writes in *Problems of Dostoevsky's Poetics*, "Nothing conclusive has yet taken place in the world, the ultimate word of the world and about the world has not yet been spoken, the world is open and free, everything is still in the future and will always be in the future" (p. 166). Life is riddled with surpluses, remainders, loopholes, and anomalies that keep things unfinalizable and therefore always hold open the possibility of surprise, change, and revolution. In this respect unfinalizability might be understood as that which undermines theoretism.

Related to unfinalizability is Bakhtin's theory of dialogism and dialogical truth, initially discussed in *Problems of Dostoevsky's Poetics* (see also his essay from the same period on "The Problem of Content," reprinted in his *Art and Answerability*). Whereas his earlier work focuses on the formation of the subject as an unfinalizable complex of identities, desires, and voices, his theory of dialogism focuses on discourse and language. **Dialogism** conceives of all discourse, in literature and in speech, as dialogical, that is, an intersection of multiple voices. When someone speaks and writes, her words are not simply streaming forth from within herself as sole author and source. Rather, her discourse, like her identity, is essentially a merger of the many voices and languages that constitute her as a subject. Every subject is made up of multiple voices, past and present, being a space of dialogue. One's speech and writing comes from that dialogical space. It is this theory of dialogism that **KRISTEVA** used to develop her theory of intertextuality, which conceives of every text and every discourse as a dialogical space, an "intersection of textual surfaces" ("Word, Dialogue, and Novel," p. 65).

So too with regard to what Bakhtin describes as "**dialogical truth**." He identifies two kinds of discourse about truth: monological and dialogical. As the word implies, monological truth is presented as a single voice. It is one with itself and allows for no contradiction, no countervoice, like a declaration from the Pope or the President. It is presented as though it is the final word— impossible as that may be. Dialogical truth, on the other hand, is the "truth" that emerges in the midst of several unmerged voices. It is an undirected intersection of voices manifesting a "plurality of consciousnesses" that does not join together in one monologic voice. It is unsystematizable, unfinalizable. The "truth" of dialogical truth is not some particular statement about what is true and what is false, but rather the particularity and uniqueness of the event itself. It is not the unity of a system but the unity of a dynamic event, a dialogue that involves struggle and contradiction.

In *Problems of Dostoevsky's Poetics*, Bakhtin focuses on dialogism in literature. Most literary presentations of dialogue, Bakhtin readily concedes, are really presenting not dialogism but a series of monologic voices. Nonetheless he insists on the power of novelistic literature to be truly dialogical (as in Dostoevsky), drawing in multiple voices without subordinating them to any one voice, creating a space of interplay in which the reader becomes a participant who must negotiate among these voices.

Another Bakhtinian concept that has gained much attention from scholars in a wide range of disciplines is **carnival**, an idea discussed in *Rabelais and His World*. Carnivals are playful subversions of the established social and political order of things, which might otherwise appear fixed. Through common practices of masquerade, the burning of effigies, the desecration of sacred objects and spaces, and excessive indulgences of the body, carnivals loosen the hold of the dominant order, breaking free—though only for a time—from law, tradition, and all that enforces normative social behavior. In Bakhtin's thinking about carnival time, as throughout his work, we recognize his insistent attention to those aspects of life and language that underscore unfinalizability, keeping people and societies open to creative transformation—something that may have seemed particularly important in Stalinist Russia.

Within the field of religious studies, Bakhtin's theories of carnival and dialogism have enjoyed considerable influence. Given his literary orientation, it is not surprising that he has been particularly influential among scholars of literature and theology as well as biblical literature. Kenneth Craig, for example, explores the Book of Esther (and, to a lesser extent, the Jewish festival of Purim based on that book) in terms of Bakhtin's concept of carnival. Other biblical scholars have engaged Bakhtin in order to develop a theory of biblical literature as fundamentally dialogical and have explored the implications of such an understanding for how scholars should approach it as well as how it functions within particular religious communities of interpretation.

One of the most important engagements of Bakhtin's work in religious studies to date is Carol A. Newsom's *The Book of Job: A Contest of Moral Imaginations* (2003). The literary complexity of the biblical book of Job has been largely understood by scholars as a dis-unity, an accruement of literary layers and voices over time that has resulted in a rather messy compilation. Thus, the beginning point for most scholars has been archeological, dismantling the text and separating its various literary layers in order to reconstruct the history of how it came to us in the form we now have it. Thus, scholars have taken a monological approach, trying to isolate each voice within the text. Drawing from Bakhtin's theories of dialogism and dialogical truth, Newsom comes to a new understanding of the literary-aesthetic unity of the Book of Job in its present form. This text, she proposes, is a dialogical space. Its unity is not monologic. On the contrary, its unity is to be found precisely in its cacophony of voices. Job is an endless and ultimately unfinalizable moral discourse on piety, suffering, and the nature of God. It is an event of moral dialogue and not a system. No one voice triumphs. As such, the "polyphonic author" of Job engages the reader in active negotiation among the voices.

Beyond its obvious contribution to biblical studies, Newsom's reading of Job, via Bakhtin, as an unfinalizable, dialogical religious discourse is suggestive for thinking about the social and cultural construction of religious communities as dialogical spaces rather than monological unities. In this light, we might conceive of a religious community not monologically, in terms of their shared system of beliefs or claims about the truth, but dialogically, in terms of dynamic, ever-changing, open-ended collections of voices in relation and in tension with one another around particular issues and questions. A religious community, like the religious text of Job, is a dialogical space.

Further Reading

By Bakhtin

Art and Answerability: Early Philosophical Essays. Edited by Michael Holquist and Vadim Liapunov. Translated by Vadim Liapunov. Austin: University of Texas Press, 1990.

Speech Genres and Other Late Essays. Edited by Caryl Emerson and Michael Holquist. Translated by Vern W. McGee. Austin: University of Texas Press, 1986.

Problems of Dostoevsky's Poetics. Edited and translated by Caryl Emerson. Minneapolis: University of Minnesota Press, 1984.

*The Dialogic Imagination: Four Essays. Edited by Michael Holquist. Translated by Caryl Emerson and Michael Holquist. Austin: University of Texas Press, 1981.

Rabelais and His World. Translated By Helene Iswolsky. Cambridge: MIT Press, 1968.

About Bakhtin

Beal, Timothy K. "Ideology and Intertextuality: Surplus of Meaning and Controlling the Means of Production." In *Reading Between Texts: Intertextuality and the Hebrew Bible*, edited by Danna Nolan Fewell. Louisville: Westminster/John Knox Press, 1992.

Boyarin, Daniel. *Intertextuality and the Reading of Midrash.* Bloomington: Indiana University Press, 1994.

Clark, Katerina, and Michael Holquist. *Mikhail Bakhtin.* Cambridge: Harvard University Press, 1984.

Coates, Ruth. *Christianity in Bakhtin: God and the Exiled Author.* Cambridge: Cambridge University Press, 1998.

Kristeva, Julia. "Word, Dialogue, and Novel." Translated by Alice Jardine, Thomas Gora, and Leon Rudiez. In *The Kristeva Reader*, edited by Toril Moi. New York: Columbia University Press, 1986.

Lock, Charles. "Carnival and Incarnation: Bakhtin and Orthodox Theology." *Literature and Theology* 5 (1991): 68–82.

*Morson, G.S., and C. Emerson. *Mikhail Bakhtin: Creation of a Prosiacs.* Stanford: Stanford University Press, 1990.

*Newsom, Carol A. "Bakhtin, the Bible, and Dialogic Truth." *Journal of Religion* 76 (1996): 290–306.

———. *The Book of Job: A Contest of Moral Imagination.* Oxford: Oxford University Press, 2002.

Pechey, Graham. "Not the Novel: Bakhtin, Poetry, Truth, God." In *Bakhtin and Cultural Theory*, edited by Ken Hirschkop and David Shepherd. New York: Palgrave, 2001.

Reed, Walter L. *Dialogues of the Word: The Bible as Literature According to Bakhtin.* Oxford: Oxford University Press, 1993.

Tull, Patricia K. "Rhetorical Criticism and Intertextuality." In *To Each Its Own Meaning: An Introduction to Biblical Criticisms and Their Applications*, edited by Stephen L. McKenzie and Stephen R. Haynes. Louisville: Westminster/John Knox Press, 1999.

ROLAND BARTHES

Key Concepts

- intertextuality
- the death of the author
- work versus text (textuality)

Roland Barthes (1915–80) was a French literary critic and cultural theorist. Born in 1915 in Cherbourg, France, he studied French and Classics at the Sorbonne in Paris. He was active in protests against fascism and wrote for leftist journals and magazines. During World War II, he taught in Paris, having been exempted from military service because of tuberculosis. After the war he taught in Romania, but later returned to school at the University of Alexandria where he studied linguistics with A. J. Greimas. He returned to Paris in the 1950s and worked at the Centre national de la recherche scientifique as a lexicographer and later as a sociologist. From 1960 until his death he taught at the École practique des hautes études. In 1976 he was elected to a chair in literary semiology at the Collège de France. Along with several others discussed in this book, he was a member of the 1960s group organized around the literary journal *Tel Quel*. Barthes died in 1980 from injuries suffered when he was struck by a van while walking in Paris.

Barthes' intellectual career can be divided into two main parts. The first consists of structuralist interpretations of both popular culture and literature. This work was particularly informed by semiotics (i.e., the study of symbol systems) and based on Saussure's theory of the linguistic sign as an arbitrary signifier whose meaning is determined in relation to and over against other signs within the system. His early work was not only influenced by but also innovative within the field of structuralist analysis. His 1957 work, *Mythologies*, for instance, made a semiotic study of popular culture and everyday life, including analyses of sign systems found in such cultural forms as advertisements, fashion, and film (see also his 1964 essay, "Introduction to the Structural Analysis of Narratives").

Beginning in the late 1960s, Barthes turned away from structuralist analysis toward poststructuralism and deconstruction (see **DERRIDA**). During this latter period, Barthes developed and expanded on ideas that have significant implications for reading texts, including religious ones.

Here we will focus on Barthes' theoretical work during this second part of his career, especially two key short essays: "The Death of the Author" (1968) and "From Work to Text" (1971). In these articles—commonly regarded as marking his poststructural turn—Barthes delineates ideas that have impacted not only the way we read particular literary texts but also the way we understand the nature of textuality and interpretation in general. These two articles question traditional, commonsense conceptions of the role of the author and the reader, and explore differences in meaning and significance of a "work" and a "text." In them, Barthes provides a critique of what are often understood as "natural" ways of reading and the "normal" relationship that exists between author, reader, and text.

"The Death of the Author" is Barthes' critique of traditional conceptions of the author, the literary work, and reading. In effect, it is a critique of the realist notion of representation, which views language as unproblematically providing an accurate depiction of reality. Barthes challenges the assumption that reality is more or less fixed, stable, and representable by language.

Barthes questions the modernist strategy of looking at an author's life and body of work in order to discern the meaning of a particular text. In this, Barthes is also critiquing his own earlier work, as in *Mythologies*, which treated cultural forms primarily as distinct and isolated from the larger world. Against this tendency to locate the meaning of a text in the intentions of its author, Barthes argues that texts can only be understood in relation to other texts. This is the notion of **intertextuality**, a term originally coined by his student and colleague Julia **KRISTEVA** (see also **BAKHTIN**'s concept of dialogism). For Barthes, as for Kristeva, every text is part of a larger field of texts that provides its context of meaning. Every text is in dialogue with other texts. Meaning, therefore, is derived not from authorial intention but from the network of relations between the reader, the text, and the larger conceptual networks suggested by that text. It is on this basis that he announces **the death of the author**, echoing Nietzsche's pronouncement of the death of God decades earlier: "The birth of the reader must be at the cost of the death of the Author" ("The Death of the Author," p. 148).

Barthes' declaration that the author is dead is not merely an obituary for the old way of understanding textual meaning. Rather, it has important ramifications for where we understand meaning to reside. Remarking on the traditional understanding of the role of the author in transmitting textual meaning, Barthes observes: "The explanation of a work is always sought in the man or woman who produced it, as if it were always in the end, through the more or less transparent allegory of the fiction, the voice of a single person, the author 'confiding' in us" ("The Death of the Author," p. 143). With the death of the author a text becomes untethered from its author such that the author can no longer be considered the transcendent source of meaning of a text and the authority for how a text must be interpreted. Contrary to conventional views, texts do not transmit a singular, fixed meaning knowable by knowing the author's life history, cultural context, or intentions.

Referring to the author to obtain textual meaning serves to legitimate one's interpretation. As long as the authority of the author holds hegemonic sway, no other interpretation can be allowed or considered. But with the author symbolically dead, interpretation can move beyond the limitations of an author-centered way of reading. Barthes argues that "[o]nce the Author is removed, the claim to decipher a text becomes quite futile. To give a text an Author is to impose a limit on that text, to furnish it with a final signified, to close the writing" ("The Death of the Author," p. 147). Thus for Barthes, removing the author and "refusing to assign a 'secret', an ultimate meaning, to the text (and to the world as text), liberates what may be called an anti-theological activity, an activity that is truly revolutionary since to refuse to fix meaning is, in the end, to refuse God and his hypostases—reason, science, law" ("The Death of the Author," p. 147).

The death of the author means the intertextualizing of the text and the rise of the reader as the interpreter. The reader now has a more important role to play in generating textual meaning because the reader is now free to interpret a text regardless of authorial intention. We, as readers, have no access to what Barthes calls the "writer's interiority." In other words, we cannot know with any certitude an author's intentions in order to locate and fix a singular textual meaning. The import of this is that it frees interpretation from the notion of a singular, authoritative meaning that has ideological and hegemonic implications. Textual interpretation shifts to the reader's interpretation of the meaning of the linguistic signs in the text. An example of this style of poststructuralist reading appears in Barthes' book-length analysis of a Balzac short story in *S/Z*.

Barthes argues that texts never convey a single meaning, but are subject to multiple meanings and interpretations. These different interpretations are not merely the result of different readers with different perspectives, but rather primarily the result of the unstable and shifting meanings of words themselves, as well as the presence of innumerable intertexts. Words are unstable because they have meaning only in relationship to other words, and because the linguistic sign is both arbitrary and differential. It is this inherent instability of language that gives rise to multiple and competing interpretations of what a text means. This view of the linguistic sign is at once an assault on traditional views of representation because it repudiates the idea of a one-to-one relationship between word (signifier) and some external, fixed meaning in the world (signified).

For Barthes, then, all texts are intertextual. That is, they are embedded in a larger system of interrelationships among multiple texts existing within a cultural context. These texts—whether fiction or nonfiction, scientific or religious, whatever textual genre—are a part of every other text, and each text is "a multidimensional space in which a variety of writings, none of them original, blend and clash" ("The Death of the Author," p. 146). Further, the multiplicity of intertextuality is located in the reader:

> Thus is revealed the total existence of writing: a text is made of multiple writings, drawn from many cultures and entering into mutual relations of dialogue, parody, contestation, but there is one place where this multiplicity is focused and that place is the reader, not, as was hitherto said, the author. The reader is the space on which all the quotations that make up a writing are inscribed without any of them being lost; a text's unity lies not in its origin but in its destination. ("The Death of the Author," p.148)

In "From Work to Text" Barthes extends his poststructuralist, intertextual view of textuality by detailing the emergence of the contemporary "**text**" over against the classical "**work**." Though he does not put it this way, we might say that, for Barthes, the death of the author is also the death of the work. Barthes explains the distinction between work and text by analogy to the difference between Newtonian to Einsteinian physics. The work is like Newtonian physics in that it assumes a world that can be accurately and objectively represented. The text, on the other hand, is like Einsteinian science with its "demands that *the relativity of the frames of reference* be included in the object studied" ("From Work to Text," p. 156).

The concept of the work can be understood as a counterpart of the living author. It reflects the traditional view of writing as the product of an individual who imbues the work with meaning. The work is a stable and contained entity that can be understood through knowledge of authorial intention and historical context. The work is also unproblematically representational. That is, its words point toward an external reality. It has a center that conveys a singular, stable truth; its meaning can be contained and controlled. The work is bounded—a thing that can be held in one's hands.

Unlike the work, the meaning of a text is unstable because it is subject to the play of meanings generated by the nature of language and intertextuality. The text is made up of what Barthes termed in "The Death of the Author," p. 146 "a tissue of quotations drawn from the innumerable centres of culture". It is this understanding of a text that readers engage in order to wrestle with its many possible interpretations. If the work is a tangible thing that can be placed on a shelf, the text is to be understood rather as something indeterminate, unfixable; it is less a thing than a process of reading and interpretation. A text is multiple, contradictory, and ambiguous, and its meaning is uncontrollable. It has no center, just writing that generates more writing. It defers closure on a fixed truth or meaning. Note that in "From Work to Text," Barthes writes the term "text" with an uppercase "T"—Text—presumably to denote not a particular text but the concept of "text" or "textuality" more generally.

Barthes' theories of textuality and textual meaning open several possibilities for students of religion. For example, his insistence, along with Kristeva, that every text is fundamentally *intertextual,* a tissue of quotations drawn from innumerable other texts, cultural assumptions, and vested interests, is suggestive with regard to the ways religious communities relate to their canons of scripture. Indeed, his theory of textuality implies that the "meaning" of those scriptures will be drawn as much from that community's *contemporary* intertextual field of intentions and interests as from its *ancient* context. It suggests, in other words, that the community of readers itself will be *read into* the text and will therefore become part of its contemporary meaning. From this perspective, then, the meaning of a scripture will be not the work of an author, but the text of a community.

Further Reading

By Barthes

Elements of Semiology. Translated by Annette Lavers and Colin Smith. New York: Hill and Wang, 1968.

Mythologies. Translated by Annette Lavers. New York: Hill and Wang, 1973.

S/Z. Translated by Richard Miller. New York: Hill and Wang, 1974.

"Introduction to the Structural Analysis of Narratives." In *Image-Music-Text,* translated by Stephen Heath. New York: Hill and Wang, 1977.

*"The Death of the Author." *Image-Music-Text.* In *Image-Music-Text,* translated by Stephen Heath. New York: Hill and Wang, 1977.

*"From Work to Text." In *Image-Music-Text,* translated by Stephen Heath. New York: Hill and Wang, 1977.

About Barthes

*Culler, Jonathan. *Roland Barthes.* New York: Oxford University Press, 1983.

Hart, Kevin. "The Poetics of the Negative." In *Reading the Text: Biblical Criticism and Literary Theory*, edited by Stephen Prickett. Oxford: Blackwell, 1991.

Lavers, Annette. *Roland Barthes: Structuralism and After.* Cambridge: Harvard University Press, 1982.

Miller, Patricia Cox. "Pleasure of the Text, Text of Pleasure: Eros and Language in Origen's Commentary on the Song of Songs." *Journal of the American Academy of Religion* 54 (1986): 241–53.

Moriarty, Michael. *Roland Barthes*. Cambridge: Polity Press, 1991.

Murphy, Tim. *Nietzsche, Metaphor, Religion*. Albany: State University of New York Press, 2001.

GEORGES BATAILLE

Key Concepts

- communication
- heterology
- order of things vs order of intimacy
- search for lost intimacy
- sacrifice

George Bataille (1897–1962) was born in Puy-de-Dôme, France. Raised without any formal religious education, he converted to Roman Catholicism in 1914, at age seventeen. The zeal with which he embraced his newfound faith is evident in his first published text, lamenting the World War I bombing of the Cathedral of Notre-Dame at Reims and praying for its restoration (see Hollier, *Against Architecture*). In 1920, however, he lost his faith abruptly when, by his own account, "his Catholicism has caused a woman he has loved to shed tears" ("Autobiographical Note," p. 113). He studied paleography and library science, and worked for twenty years at the Bibliothèque nationale. In 1951 he was named conservator at Bibliothèque municipale at Orléans. In a scholarly and artistic career spanning more than four decades, he wrote on a wide range of subjects, including numismatics, eroticism (he wrote erotic fiction as well as nonfiction on the subject of eroticism), autobiography, politics, literary criticism, philosophy, sociology, and religion.

Bataille was involved in a number of short-lived, radical anti-fascist groups, including the Surrealist movement (which denounced him in its Second Surrealist Manifesto in 1929) and the Democratic Communist Circle, which published the journal *La Critique sociale* (published from 1931 to 1934). He also organized a group called Contre-Attaque (1935–36) and soon after that helped found a "secret society" which aimed to turn its back on politics and pursue goals that were solely religious—albeit "anti-Christian, essentially Nietzschean" ("Autobiographical Note," p. 115). The public face of this secret society was the now-famous Collège de sociologie and its journal *Acéphale* ("headless"), which ran from 1936 to 1939.

Although he abandoned Catholicism in his early twenties, he remained interested in religion, especially mysticism, throughout his life. For Bataille, religion was a field of activity and experience that could not be reduced to social utility or moral values. It does not simply make good workers and good citizens. There is within religion an impulse toward excess and extravagance that belies its orientation toward otherness and reveals its potential for subversion of social order.

In all of his work, Bataille sought human experiences that reveal the limits of thought, "other" experiences beyond representation in language—the burst of laughter, erotic love, potlatch, sacrifice, mystical union. He sought to highlight those experiences that exceed independent self-existence, experiences of disorientation and unknowing that shatter the self. Such experiences, Bataille believed, are what make **communication** possible because they break open the self and put it into relation with others. The disintegration of the self is a kind of self-transcendence (transcending the self as a discrete body and mind) that opens one to the possibility of communion with others. In *On Nietzsche*, Bataille describes the Christian story of the crucifixion of Christ as a radical act of communication: a self-laceration of the divine that opens toward communion with all human beings.

In an early essay called "The Use-Value of D.A.F. de Sade (An Open Letter to My Current Comrades)," written in 1929 or 1930, Bataille proposes a new academic program of study that focuses on this "other scene" of subversive excess, rupture, and self-transcendence. He calls this program **heterology**, defined as "the science of what is completely other" (*hetero* = "other") ("Use-Value," note 2). Indeed, heterology is an apt description of Bataille's entire life's work. Heterology attends to that which is other and therefore accursed within the dominant social order because it cannot be assimilated into it. It deals with that which is useless in a world driven by use-value and that which is wasteful in a world driven by production; it is what is pronounced evil in a world that reduces the sacred to moral goodness.

Bataille's heterology has a strong if unorthodox orientation toward the religious. The "completely other" that is the focus of heterology is, for Bataille, closely related to notions of the "sacred"—but not as it is commonly associated in contemporary Western religious discourse with goodness (versus evil) and reverence. Rather, he understands the sacred as fundamentally ambivalent: on the one hand, set apart as holy and revered; on the other hand, set apart as accursed and dirty. In a footnote, he writes that *agiology*—from the Greek *agio*, "holy" or "sacred"—might be a more appropriate term than heterology, "but one would have to catch the double meaning of *agio* (analogous to the double meaning of *sacer* [sacred]), *soiled* as well as *holy*" ("Use-Value," note 2).

Elsewhere in the essay he equates the "completely other" of the numinous, the wholly other, the unknowable, the sacr? religious. He even considers whether his program should b rather than "heterology," but is concerned that "religion" i? society is too closely associated with institutions that regulate an? access to the sacred.

Unlike other theorists discussed in this book, Bataille developed a full-blown theory of religion (*Theory of Religion*; first published in French in 1973, though written years earlier), which is closely related to his better known three-volume *The Accursed Share*. In *Theory of Religion*, Bataille conceives of two radically opposed regions or "worlds": the order of intimacy and the order of things.

The **order of intimacy**—also described by Bataille as the sacred world—is the realm of undivided continuity and flow in which there are no distinct objects or individual selves, an "opaque aggregate" (p. 36) reminiscent of the primordial chaos described in many creation mythologies. (This is also reminiscent of **LACAN**'s prelinguistic stage before individuation and subject formation, the Imaginary.) In intimacy, there is no self-consciousness of oneself as an individual in relation to other individuals and objects. Bataille associates this realm with animality, for animals are "*in the world like water in water . . . the animal, like the plant, has no autonomy in relation to the rest of the world*" (p. 19).

The **order of things**, which he also calls the profane or ordinary world, is the order of discontinuity, individuation, division, and subdivision into subjects and objects. Whereas the order of intimacy is a realm of animality, the order of things is a realm of humanity. An early step out of the animal order of intimacy and into the human order of things was made when we began to use tools. A tool (a rock for hammering, a sharp stick for hunting) is something that we set apart and treat as an object, thereby positing ourselves as a subject. Thus the tool object and the tool-using subject are separated out of the undifferentiated continuity of intimacy and transformed into "things." We use the tool, moreover, to make and manipulate still other objects. In the process, we are self-objectifying, positing ourselves as an object in a world of other objects.

We experience this order of things, the "world of things and bodies," as the profane or ordinary world—"this world"—set over against a "holy and mythical world" of intimacy. The two worlds are incommensurable. "Nothing, as a matter of fact, is more closed to us than this animal life from which we are descended" (p. 20). So the order of intimacy, which is lost to us, is this world's wholly other, which is "vertiginously dangerous for that clear and profane world where mankind situates its privileged domain" (p. 36).

The privileged human domain of the order of things separates us from the order of intimacy and keeps it at bay—keeps it from breaking in and returning the order of things to primordial undifferentiated chaos.

[Humankind] is afraid of the intimate order that is not reconcilable with the order of things. . . . [I]ntimacy, in the trembling of the individual, is holy, sacred, and suffused with anguish. . . . The sacred is that prodigious effervescence of life that, for the sake of duration, the order of things holds in check and that this holding changes into a breaking loose, that is, into violence. It constantly threatens to break the dikes, to confront productive activity with the precipitate and contagious movement of a purely glorious consumption. (pp. 52–53)

What is religion in relation to these two worlds? According to Bataille, religion is "**the search for lost intimacy**" (p. 57). While occupying the order of things, it reaches for contact with the order of intimacy. It operates according to the desire to commune with the wholly other sacred world of intimacy while remaining part of the order of things. It is in this world but not of it. In his characteristic heterodox way, Bataille also associates erotic desire with religious desire in many of his writings, especially *Erotism* (first published in French in 1957). The lover's desire for intimate communion with another is, for Bataille, the desire to lose one's individual selfhood, to dissolve in intimacy.

Within religion, Bataille presents **sacrifice** as an exemplary expression of this desire for lost intimacy. For Bataille, sacrifice is a failed effort at crossing over from the order of things to the intimate order. Rituals of sacrifice (*sacri-facere*, "to make sacred") take something with use-value within the order of things (a domestic animal, a person, a bushel of grain), removes it from that order, and passes it over to the order of intimacy, that is, to the realm of the sacred, through an act of wasteful consumption (burning, orgiastic feasting, etc.). Sacrifice is about wasting something that has use-value within the order of things, thereby sending it over to the other side, to the sacred realm of intimacy. This is why sacrificial animals are domestic rather than wild: a wild animal is already in the order of intimacy.

According to this idea of sacrifice, festival, carnival, and potlatch are also sacrificial practices. They are acts of sacred waste, removing valuables from the order of things by excessive (and therefore wasteful) consumption, and also, in the case of carnival, ruining social capital by mocking or otherwise subverting figures of public authority and law.

For Bataille, then, the religious violence of sacrifice must be distinguished from other kinds of violence, such as war. Contrary to patriotic proclamations that a soldier's death in battle is a sacrifice for a sacred cause (God, nation, capitalism), casualties of war are not sacrificial because they serve some cause deemed socially valuable. In war, the things and bodies that a people or nation expend are the price paid for advancing or maintaining some value within the order of things.

As in his earlier work on heterology, Bataille's description of the sacred world of intimacy as "vertiginously dangerous" leads to an understanding of religious experience—that is, experience of the sacred—as an irreducible combination of fascination and repulsion, fear and desire (vertigo: the experience of feeling simultaneously pulled over the edge and pulled back from it). As he writes in the second volume of *The Accursed Share*, "It is obviously the combination of abhorrence and desire that gives the sacred world a paradoxical character, holding one who considers it without cheating in a state of anxious fascination" (p. 95). Here we are reminded of Rudolph Otto's well-known characterization of religious experience as an encounter with the *Mysterium tremendum et fascinans*, a wholly other that is both terrifying and fascinating.

Despite the fact that Bataille rightly passes as a theorist of religion, his work has had relatively little influence on the field of religious studies, especially among those working in English. This lack of influence is partly due to his unorthodox writing style, which often mixes traditional forms of academic argument with aphorism and autobiography, and partly due to the fact that many of his works on religion were not translated into English until the late 1980s. Two exceptions are worth noting here, insofar as each represents a particularly fruitful area for further scholarship on Bataille and religion.

First, in the field of religion and culture, Andrew Wernick, in "Bataille's Columbine: The Sacred Space of Hate" (1999), has interpreted the 1999 massacre/suicide at Columbine High School in Colorado in light of Bataille's conceptions of heterology and sacrifice. He argues that this outbreak of apparently meaningless violence indicates the rise in American youth culture of a new "heterological activism" driven by a desire to bring forth "what is absolutely unassimilable to the ruling order." Contrary to other interpretations of this event, Wernick draws on Bataille, as well as Jean **BAUDRILLARD**, to argue that this act of violence was meant to be meaningless, wasteful, without purpose. It was meaningless slaughter. As such, it was, in Bataille's sense, a kind of sacrifice. "The intent . . . was to kill everyone. Or, to put it differently: it was to immolate the community of Columbine High—themselves included—as a whole."

Second, in the field of biblical studies and theology, Tod Linafelt, in "Biblical Love Poetry (. . . and God)," has brought Bataille's work on eroticism into closer relation to his work on religion vis-à-vis the Song of Songs. Although the Song of Songs is literally a love poem composed of the voices of two young lovers expressing their desire for one another, it has often been read as an allegory for human–divine love. In his work on eroticism, Bataille argues that divine love is not a desire for lost intimacy, as human love is, because God is never at risk, never susceptible to self-dissolution. Thus, for Bataille, carnal love is superior to divine love. On the contrary, Linafelt argues that self-dissolution is precisely what is at stake in the divine–human love relationship as represented in biblical literature and especially in Jewish and Christian devotional writings. Not only is the human at risk in this love affair, but so is God, as is most evident in the divine anguish and passion of God as represented in the images of God as lover in the biblical prophetic literature.

Further Reading
By Bataille

*The Bataille Reader, edited by Fred Botting and Scott Wilson. Oxford: Blackwell, 1997.

"Autobiographical Note." In The Bataille Reader, edited by Fred Botting and Scott Wilson. Oxford: Blackwell, 1997.

"The Use-Value of D.A.F. de Sade (An Open Letter to My Current Comrades)." Translated by Allan Stoekl with Carl R. Lovitt and Donald M. Leslie Jr. In The Bataille Reader, edited by Fred Botting and Scott Wilson. Oxford: Blackwell, 1997.

*Theory of Religion. Translated by Robert Hurley. New York: Zone, 1989.

The Accursed Share. Vol. 1, Consumption. Translated by Robert Hurley. New York: Zone, 1988.

The Accursed Share. Vol. 2, The History of Eroticism; Vol.3 Sovereignty. Translated by Robert Hurley. New York: Zone, 1991.

Inner Experience. Translated by Leslie Anne Boldt. Albany: State University of New York Press, 1988.

On Nietzsche. Translated by Bruce Boone. New York: Paragon, 1992.

Erotism: Death and Sensuality. Translated by Mary Dalwood. San Francisco: City Lights, 1986.

About Bataille

*Brown, Norman O. "Dionysus in 1990." In Apocalypse and/or Metamorphosis. Berkeley: University of California Press, 1991.

Campbell, Robert A. "Georges Bataille's Surrealistic Theory of Religion." Method & Theory in the Study of Religion 11 (1999): 127–42.

Connor, Peter. Georges Bataille and the Mysticism of Sin. Baltimore: Johns Hopkins University Press, 2000.

Gemerchak, Christopher M. The Sunday of the Negative: Reading Bataille, Reading Hegel. Albany: State University of New York Press, 2003.

Hollier, Denis. Against Architecture: The Writings of Georges Bataille. Cambridge: MIT Press, 1992.

Hollywood, Amy. "'Divine Woman/Divine Women': The Return of the Sacred in Bataille, Lacan, and Irigaray." In The Question of Christian Philosophy Today, edited Francis J. Ambrosio. New York: Fordham University Press, 2000.

*Linafelt, Tod. "Biblical Love Poetry (. . . and God)." Journal of the American Academy of Religion 70 (2002): 323–45.

Murphy, Tim. "Bataille, Theory, and Politics: A Response to Carl Olson." Method & Theory in the Study of Religion 8 (1996): 361–66.

Olson, Carl. "Eroticism, Violence, and Sacrifice: A Postmodern Theory of Religion and Ritual." Method & Theory in the Study of Religion 6 (1994): 231–50.

Wernick, Andrew. "Bataille's Columbine: The Sacred Space of Hate." CTheory.Net, November 1999. <www.ctheory.net>.

JEAN BAUDRILLARD

Key Concepts

- simulation
- simulacra
- the postmodern
- hyperreality

Jean Baudrillard (1929–) is a postmodern cultural theorist who is particularly noted for his critiques of contemporary consumer society. Trained as a sociologist, he has become one of the key theorists of postmodernity.

Baudrillard was born in 1929 in Reims in northeastern France. His grandparents were peasant farmers and his parents worked in civil service jobs. At the University of Nanterre, he studied sociology under Henri **LEFEBVRE**. He taught sociology at Nanterre from 1966 until his retirement in 1987. His earliest work was written from the perspective of a Marxist sociologist, but in subsequent studies his intellectual mentors often came to be the objects of his critiques, including Lefebvre, Marx, and Sartre. Baudrillard's early engagement with Marxist theory was later abandoned after he embraced poststructuralist ideas in the 1970s. Baudrillard was also a student of the theories of Roland **BARTHES** and the mass media theorist Marshall McLuhan. Baudrillard's first book, *The System of Objects* (published in French in 1968), is a semiotic analysis of culture that was influenced by Barthes' poststructuralist ideas.

Baudrillard's work on postmodern culture—usually radical in its claims—utilizes ideas drawn from various disciplines including linguistics, philosophy, sociology, and political science. He addresses a wide range of issues, including mass media, mass consumption, consumer society, war, and terrorism. Baudrillard is best known for work such as *Simulacra and Simulation* (published in French in 1981), in which he analyzes the nature of postmodern culture, asserting that contemporary culture can no longer distinguish image from reality. Baudrillard's view is that the "conventional universe of subject and object, of ends and means, of good and bad, does not correspond any more to the state of our world" (*Impossible Exchange*, p. 28).

Within the context of his explorations of postmodern Western culture, Baudrillard is especially interested in representation. His work examines ways in which technology and media impact how we represent our experiences and what we can know about the world. Baudrillard argues that contemporary culture is so saturated with images from television, film, advertising, and other forms of mass media that differences between the real and the imagined, or truth and falsity, are indistinguishable. Images do not represent reality, but rather become reality. Our lives are thus **simulations** of reality in the sense that simulation constructs what counts as the real from conceptualizations that have no intrinsic or direct connection to reality. Images produced by mass media neither refer to reality nor harbor any independent meaning.

What are the implications of living in an image-saturated, postmodern society? In effect, our experiences of the world are mediated through the many images that confront us every day and that frame how we see the world and what we see. Notions of the perfect body, for instance, come about not because of some unmediated experience we have in the world, but largely through all the body images projected by media, advertising, and other instruments of image production.

Central to Baudrillard's understanding of the relationship between reality and representations of it are the concepts of "simulacrum" and "hyperreality." A **simulacrum** is an image or representation of something. Baudrillard uses this term to refer to an image that has *replaced* the thing it supposedly represents. In *Simulacra and Simulation*, Baudrillard distinguishes three phases, or "orders," of the simulacrum in Western history. With each order, the image or simulacrum is increasingly alienated from that which it purports to represent. First-order simulacra, which alter or mask reality, emerge prominently in the baroque period, with its privileging of artifice over realism. Drawing from Walter **BENJAMIN**'s essay, "The Work of Art in the Age of Mechanical Reproduction," Baudrillard identifies the emergence of second-order simulacra with the modern age of mass production and its resulting proliferation of reproductions, that is, images of an "original" image, which in turn is an image of the "real" thing. It is an image of an image. Third-order simulacra are the simulacra of the current **postmodern** age. In postmodernity, the simulacrum has lost all relation to reality. It is a production of reality, not an imitation. In postmodernity, the simulacrum has replaced the real so that we live in a world of simulacra.

Although images may appear to refer to or represent objects in the real world, "reflecting" a preexisting reality, Baudrillard argues that in postmodernity images precede the real. If so, then we live in a world of simulation and not of reality. One characteristic of such a postmodern world is the proliferation of media for producing images that simulate reality, including photography, film, television, and the World Wide Web. Baudrillard says, "To simulate is to feign to have what one doesn't have" (*Simulacra and Simulation*, p. 3). In short, simulation does not refer to reality or pretend to imitate it; rather, it constructs reality.

In *Simulacra and Simulation*, Baudrillard provides us with an example of how an image becomes reality itself. He cites a Jorge Luis Borges story in which "the cartographers of the Empire draw up a map so detailed that it ends up covering the territory exactly" (*Simulacra and Simulation*, p. 1). The map, which is a representation of a real space, becomes the reality, or, to use Baudrillard's term, a **hyperreality**: "Simulation is no longer that of a territory, a referential being, or a substance. It is the generation by models of a real without origin or reality: a hyperreal" (*Simulacra and Simulation*, p. 1). From this perspective, "[t]he territory no longer precedes the map, nor does it survive it. It is nevertheless the map that precedes the territory—*precession of simulacra*—that engenders the territory, and if one must return to the fable, today it is the territory whose shreds slowly rot across the extent of the map" (*Simulacra and Simulation*, p. 1). For Baudrillard, the map has become the reality, not a representation of it. A hyperreal world, then, is one in which the real and the imaginary have imploded and the boundaries separating them no longer stand, nor do boundaries separating autonomous spheres exist. Thus, for instance, CNN and other cable news networks blur distinctions between fact, opinion, sports, politics, weather, and entertainment. The news does not describe or represent reality, it is reality. Baudrillard goes so far as to argue that media and other imaginary constructs, like Disneyland, function to create America itself as nothing more than a hyperreal simulation of the real.

Simulation commonly refers to something fake or counterfeit, unreal or inauthentic. But Baudrillard does not simply contrast simulation with the real; rather, he sees these as having suffered a radical disconnection. For Baudrillard, we can no longer meaningfully inquire about the relative truth or falsity of images and representations. Virtual worlds created by computer graphics underscore the idea that a reality can be created where there is no preexisting reality that the virtual version represents.

Baudrillard's ideas raise significant questions and issues for the study of religion. The proliferation of images that, he asserts, characterizes the postmodern is also characteristic of at least some forms of contemporary religion and the technologies used by these religions to promote and disseminate their messages. How, we might ask, does the proliferation of images by various media affect religion? Has contemporary religion become a simulation of religions past? If so, how? How does TV evangelism, for instance, take advantage of the saturation of images in a postmodern world? Are religious representations ever really anything other than simulations? These Baudrillardian questions and issues are all the more intriguing given the notion that religion is typically understood to describe the "really" real—a reality that Baudrillard claims no longer exists.

Further Reading
By Baudrillard

*The Transparency of Evil: Essays on Extreme Phenomena. Translated by James Benedict. London: Verso, 1993.

*Simulacra and Simulation. Translated by Sheila Faria Glaser. Ann Arbor: University of Michigan Press, 1994.

Impossible Exchange. Translated by Chris Turner. London: Verso, 2001.

Jean Baudrillard: Selected Writings. 2nd ed. Edited by Mark Poster. Stanford: Stanford University Press, 2001.

About Baudrillard

Bennett-Carpenter, Benjamin. "The Divine Simulacrum of Andy Warhol: Baudrillard's Light on the Pope of Pop's 'Religious Art.'" Journal for Cultural and Religious Theory 1, no. 3 (2001). <www.jcrt.org/archives/01.3/carpenter.shtml>.

Caputo , John D. "For Love of the Things Themselves: Derrida's Hyper-Realism." Journal for Cultural and Religious Theory 1, no. 3 (2001). <www.jcrt.org/archives/01.3/caputo.shtml>.

Detweiler, Robert. "Apocalyptic Fiction and the End(s) of Realism." In European Literature and Theology in the Twentieth Century, edited by David Jasper and Colin Crowder. New York: Palgrave 1990.

Horrocks, Chris, and Zoran Jevtic. Introducing Baudrillard. Lanham: Totem Books, 1996.

*Kellner, Douglas. Jean Baudrillard: From Marxism to Postmodernism and Beyond. Stanford: Stanford University Press, 1989.

*Lane, Richard J. Jean Baudrillard. London and New York: Routledge, 2000.

Raschke, Carl. "The Deposition of the Sign: Postmodernism and the Crisis of Religious Studies." Journal for Cultural and Religious Theory 3, no. 1 (2002). <www.jcrt.org/ archives/03.1/ raschke.shtml>.

Smith, M. W. Reading Simulacra: Fatal Theories for Postmodernity. Albany: State University of New York Press, 2001.

Wernick, Andrew. "Post-Marx: Theological Themes in Baudrillard's America." In Shadow of Spirit: Postmodernism and Religion, edited by Philippa Berry and Andrew Wernick. London and New York: Routledge, 1992.

Wernick, Andrew. "Jean Baudrillard: Seducing God." Post-secular Philosophy: Between Philosophy and Theology. Edited by Phillip Blond. London and New York: Routledge, 1998.

WALTER BENJAMIN

Key Concepts

- critique of violence
- the task of the translator
- the work of art in the age of mechanical reproduction
- angel of history

Walter Benjamin (1892–1940) was born in Berlin to a Jewish family that had largely assimilated to the city's Christian mainstream. He was educated at the universities of Berlin, Freiburg, Munich, and Bern. As a student he became involved in radical Jewish student movements and, along with his close friend Gershom Scholem, grew increasingly interested in Jewish mysticism. (Scholem went on to become a great scholar of Jewish mysticism.) In 1925 Benjamin submitted *The Origin of German Tragic Drama* as his *Habilitationsschrift* (a document required for promotion to a university position) at the University of Frankfurt. It was rejected because of its unconventional, lyrical style, and Benjamin never held a formal academic post. He worked as an independent scholar, freelance critic, and translator.

In 1933, with the rise of the Nazis in Germany, Benjamin moved to Paris, where he met Hannah Arendt among many other intellectuals. In 1939 he was deprived of his German nationality and spent time in an internment camp. In 1940, at the invitation of Theodor Adorno and Max Horkheimer of the School for Social Research (recently moved from Frankfurt to New York to escape the Nazis), Benjamin attempted to flee the French Vichy regime for the United States. When he arrived at Portbou on the Franco-Spanish border, he was refused entry into Spain. To return to France would have meant certain death. The next morning he was found dead, apparently a suicide by morphine overdose.

Benjamin wrote on a wide range of topics—from literary tragedy to modernity to Paris to messianism—and in a range of styles, from essay to commentary to aphorism. Artists, historians, literary critics and philosophers have all been drawn to his texts for their insight and provocation. With regard to the academic study of religion, his work in critical theory is particularly valuable because of the questions it raises about origins and foundations. Here we will focus on four particular pieces: "Critique of Violence" (1921), "The Task of the Translator" (1923), "The Work of Art in the Age of Mechanical Reproduction" (1936), and his parable on the angel of history from "Theses on the Philosophy of History" (1940).

In "**Critique of Violence**," Benjamin examines the foundations of law, or lack thereof. The law, he argues, cannot stand on its own. It has no foundation (in divine commandment, in nature, etc.). If it did, then it would not be necessary to resort to violence in order to establish and maintain itself. Indeed, its utter reliance on violence reveals the fact that it is, in itself, groundless. Where there should be a foundation, there is only violence. The usual approach to justifying violence within the legal system turns our attention away from this fact, insofar as it focuses on justifying legal violence (imposing and preserving the law) in terms of the ends justifying the means: if the end is deemed just, then so is the violent means necessary to achieve that end. Thus, Benjamin argues, we are distracted from asking what the necessity of legal violence might reveal about the law itself, namely the law's own lack of any solid foundation. The law in itself is not enough; it can't stand on its own. It must resort to violence in order to establish and perpetuate itself. Violence is located where law's foundation should be.

In "**The Task of the Translator**" (an introduction to his translation of Baudelaire's *Tableaux Parisiens*), Benjamin pushes this questioning of origins and foundations in a very different direction, exploring the relation between an original literary work and its "afterlife" in translation. What is it that is being translated? With regard to any literary work worth translating, it is not simply information but "the unfathomable, the mysterious, the 'poetic,' something that a translator can reproduce only if he is also a poet" (p. 70). Translation is an art by which a literary work becomes something more than itself. In translation, the work has an "afterlife," which is something more than it was originally. Translation is a "stage of continued life." Therefore, in the work of the translator, the original work must die to itself in order to live beyond itself in another language as a work of literary art. At the same time, the original *calls for* its translation because it, in itself, is incomplete and ultimately cannot reach the unfathomable mystery it seeks to attain. The task of the translator is not simply to convey the original's information to those who can't read the original's language. Rather, it is a task of "recreation" aimed at liberating the poetic power of the text from its imprisonment within a particular (and necessarily non-universal, impure) language (p. 80).

In *Surviving Lamentations: Catastrophe, Lament, and Protest in the Afterlife of a Biblical Book* (2000), Tod Linafelt explores the "afterlife" of the biblical book of Lamentations (lament poetry concerning the destruction of Jerusalem by the Babylonians), demonstrating the power of Benjamin's understanding of translation for studying the history of biblical interpretation. He shows how the original text of Lamentations, especially in its unfathomable voice of suffering and the striking lack of divine response, calls for its own translation, that is, its own afterlife. Linafelt reads the translations, interpretations, poetry, and fiction that follow Lamentations as the book's afterlife, a literature of survival (*survival*, "over-living" or "living beyond") that tries—and inevitably fails—to recreate and liberate the voice of suffering in that original text.

Benjamin's now classic 1936 essay, "**The Work of Art in the Age of Mechanical Reproduction**," explores the origins of the work of art in relation to what he believes to be a radically new era in art history brought on by new methods of mass reproduction. Important here is the concept of "authenticity," by which Benjamin refers to the original work of art's unique existence in time and space, "where it happens to be," in other words, its "historical testimony" (p. 220). This is the essence or "aura" of the work of art that cannot be reproduced. It is what gives the original work its *distance*, its historical otherness in relation to us. Mechanical reproduction is driven by the desire to close that distance, "to get hold of an object at very close range by way of its likeness, its reproduction" (p. 223). And yet, with every reproduction, the aura of the original is diminished because "the technique of reproduction detaches the reproduced object from the domain of tradition," alienating it from its original location, thereby substituting "a plurality of copies for a unique existence" (p. 221). Reproduction depends on that original work's aura (otherwise there would be no interest in reproducing it) even while it uproots it from the historical time and space that gives it its aura. Thus reproduction unwittingly liquidates the aura of the original work of art, substituting a simulation— a topic later explored by Jean **BAUDRILLARD**.

Benjamin further argues that the work of art's aura, its rootedness in tradition, has its basis in ritual. This, he insists, was the work of art's first and original use-value. Long before beauty or some other aesthetic experience was the artist's goal, and long before "art for art's sake," the work of art was made for use in religious ritual. As artists increasingly did their work with the explicit aim of public exhibition rather than ritual function, the work of art began to break free from its religious roots. Nonetheless, Benjamin argues, until this new age of mechanical reproduction, those roots still cohered to the work of art.

Now, however, we are for the first time witnessing the radical "emancipation" of the work of art from "its parasitical dependence on ritual" (p. 224). In this new age, artists increasingly make their works with the conscious intention of reproducing them. The original is created for the purpose of its own reproduction. The work of art's reproducibility has become paramount, leading to a qualitative transformation of the nature of art: breaking free from its original roots in ritual practice, it has the potential to serve an entirely new practice, namely politics. Benjamin sees film as the most serviceable example of this new form of reproducible art. Film has the power to "mobilize the masses" (p. 240), whether the goal is nationalism or revolution, acceptance or resistance. It does so by distracting spectators—inducing a state of absentmindedness— while at the same time reshaping their worldview, their conception of reality.

Remember that Benjamin was writing "The Work of Art in the Age of Mechanical Reproduction" in 1936 during the rise of Nazism—a movement particularly adept at art as political propaganda. Think of the pervasive graphic posters, but also nationalistic films like *Triumph of the Will*, the Nazi-funded film about the 1934 rally in Nuremburg. Benjamin's essay provokes new questions at the beginning of the twenty-first century, a time in which new media technologies are proliferating with ever increasing speed and turnover. Even if we accept Benjamin's argument, we must ask whether art in our new age of "digital reproduction," for example, is a continuation of the revolutionary age of mechanical reproduction to which he refers, or whether it somehow exceeds or overturns that age.

Scholar of religion and visual culture S. Brent Plate (*Walter Benjamin, Religion, and Aesthetics*) has drawn from Benjamin's "Work of Art" essay and other writings in order to make a case for moving the study of religious art away from its contemplative-intellectual orientation and toward the material practices of artistic production and reception. Relatedly, he argues that religion itself is not based on ideas and doctrines but on corporeal, bodily operations of the senses. Religion is fundamentally aesthetic in this sense (Greek *aisthetikos*, sense perception of material things).

As mentioned earlier, Benjamin is known not only for his essays but also for his aphoristic writings. His "Theses on the Philosophy of History" (written in 1940 but not published until 1950), is a series of brief, loosely related reflections on historical research and historiography, the relation of the present to the past, the desire for lost origins, and the idea of historical progress. The best known of his "Theses" is the ninth, a parable on the "**angel of history**." The parable is inspired by Paul Klee's painting "Angelus Novus," in which an angel appears to be flying backward, wings spread open, staring intently at something it is leaving behind. "This," Benjamin reflects, "is how one pictures the angel of history" (p. 257). Like an historian, the angel of history is looking back, face turned toward the past, as he moves through time away from it. He is flying backward into the future. Whereas we are accustomed to viewing the past as a chain of events connecting the past to the present, the angel "sees one single catastrophe which keeps piling wreckage upon wreckage and hurls it in front of his feet." The angel wants to go back and "make whole what has been smashed" (p. 257). But a storm is blowing from Paradise, that is, from the beginning of history. And its winds have caught him by his wings "with such violence that the angel can no longer close them" (p. 258). Thus as the storm blows him backwards through time, propelling him into the future, the wreckage of the past before him grows higher and higher. "This storm," Benjamin concludes, "is what we call progress" (p. 258).

Further Reading

By Benjamin

"Critique of Violence." In *Reflections*, edited by Peter Demetz and translated by Edmund Jephcott. New York: Harcourt Brace Jovanovich, 1978.

*"The Task of the Translator." In *Illuminations*, edited by Hannah Arendt and translated by Harry Zohn, New York: Harcourt, Brace and World, 1968.

*"The Work of Art in the Age of Mechanical Reproduction." In *Illuminations*, edited by Hannah Arendt and translated by Harry Zohn. New York: Harcourt, Brace and World, 1968.

"Theses on the Philosophy of History." In *Illuminations*, edited by Hannah Arendt and translated by Harry Zohn New York: Harcourt, Brace and World, 1968.

The Origin of German Tragic Drama. Translated by John Osborne. London: Verso, 1977.

The Correspondence of Walter Benjamin and Gershom Scholem, 1932–1940. Translated by Gary Smith and André Lefevere. New York: Schocken, 1989.

About Benjamin

Alter, Robert. *Necessary Angels: Traditions and Modernity in Kafka, Benjamin and Scholem*. Cambridge: Harvard University Press, 1991.

Britt, Brian M. *Walter Benjamin and the Bible*. New York: Continuum, 1996.

Davis, Charles. "Walter Benjamin, the Mystical Materialist." In *Truth and Compassion*, edited by H. Joseph, J. N. Lightstone, and M. D. Oppenheim. Waterloo: Wilfrid Laurier University Press, 1983.

*Handelman, Susan A. *Fragments of Redemption: Jewish Thought and Literary Theory in Benjamin, Scholem, and Levinas*. Bloomington: Indiana University Press, 1991.

Arendt Hannah. "Introduction" In *Illuminations*, edited by Hannah Arendt and translated by Harry Zohn. New York: Harcourt, Brace and World, 1968.

Linafelt, Tod. *Surviving Lamentations: Catastrophe, Lament, and Protest in the Afterlife of a Biblical Book*. Chicago: University of Chicago Press, 2000.

*Plate, S. Brent. *Walter Benjamin, Religion, and Aesthetics: Rethinking Religion through the Arts*. New York and London: Routledge, 2004.

Wohfarth, Irving. "On Some Jewish Motifs in Benjamin." *In The Problems of Modernity: Adorno and Benjamin*, edited by Andrew Benjamin. London and New York: Routledge, 1989.

PIERRE BOURDIEU

Key Concepts

- habitus
- doxa
- cultural capital
- taste

Pierre Bourdieu (1930–2002) was a French sociologist whose work has been widely influential in both the social sciences and humanities. He was born in rural southwestern France, where his father worked as a postal worker. Bourdieu received a scholarship that enabled him to attend the prestigious *lycée* Louis-leGrand in Paris. He subsequently enrolled at the École normale supérieure where he studied with Louis **ALTHUSSER**. After graduating with a degree in philosophy, Bourdieu taught first at the high school level. In 1959 he was appointed to a position in philosophy at the Sorbonne, after which he taught at the University of Paris from 1960 to 1964. In 1964 he was named director of studies at the École des hautes études en sciences sociales and founded the Center for the Sociology of Education and Culture. In 1982 he was named chair of sociology at the Collège de France. He received the "Medaille d'Or" (Gold Medal) from the French National Scientific Research Center in 1993.

During his military service, Bourdieu spent time teaching in Algeria. This experience made him acutely aware of the social effects of French colonialism and the social inequality embedded in such a system. He later conducted ethnographic fieldwork in Algeria. This research was the foundation for many of his concepts and theories. Bourdieu also conducted fieldwork in France, where he studied the structures of social and class differences in French society. He was interested in how systems of social inequality are embedded in cultural practices. He paid particular attention to the study of the French education system and demonstrated how it reproduced class difference despite its claims to the contrary.

Bourdieu was a public intellectual. In 2001 he became a celebrity with the appearance of a popular documentary film about him, "Sociology Is a Combat Sport." His books were often best-sellers in France. He matched his status as a public intellectual with political activism. Bourdieu was involved in fighting social injustice, publicly criticizing the inequalities in the French social class structure, and supporting better conditions for, among others, the working classes and the homeless. He was also closely associated with antiglobalization movements.

Bourdieu's large body of work—he authored more than twenty-five volumes—covers a number of different areas, including the sociology of culture and taste, education, language, literature, and cultural aspects of museums. Among his best-known texts are *Outline of a Theory of Practice* (published in French in 1972), *Distinction* (published in French in 1979), and *The Logic of Practice* (published in French in 1980). Many of his key concepts (e.g., habitus, doxa, and cultural capital) have had a significant and ongoing influence on the humanities and social sciences.

Blending structuralist perspectives on social systems with concern for individual human agency, Bourdieu seeks to understand patterns of human behavior and how they are generated by and within society. His concept of practice, developed in *Outline of a Theory of Practice*, figures significantly in how he explains the processes by which social patterns of behavior reproduce structures of domination. By practice, Bourdieu refers to the things that people *do* as opposed to what they *say*. This is related to his concern with agency: how do individuals contribute to the reproduction of social restrictions and what it is possible and not possible to do in a particular cultural context? Bourdieu develops the notion of practice through the concept of **habitus**. Bourdieu defines habitus as a system of "durable, transposable *dispositions*, structured structures predisposed to function as structuring structures, that is, as principles of the generation and structuring of practices and represen-tations which can be objectively 'regulated' and 'regular' without in any way being the product of obedience to rules" (*Outline of a Theory of Practice*, p. 72). In other words, a habitus is a set of dispositions that generate and structure human actions and behaviors. It shapes all practice, and yet it is not experienced as repressive or enforcing. Its effects on us typically go unnoticed.

A specific habitus comes into focus when social and cultural markers such as occupation, income, education, religion, and taste preferences (food, clothing, music, and art) are juxtaposed one against another. For example, a corporate executive with an advanced college degree, disposable income, season tickets to the symphony, and a taste for fine wine contrasts with the dispositions (habitus) of a "blue collar" worker with a high school diploma or G.E.D. and significant debt, who watches sports on TV and prefers Budweiser to Bordeaux.

Bourdieu locates habitus where these dispositions correlate as traits common to a particular social group or class. A specific set of such dispositions is what Bourdieu means by the term habitus.

Knowing the habitus of a particular person—what social group or class they fit into by virtue of a set of dispositions—does not provide the social scientist with predictive power to know what practices a person will engage in. To claim this would be to remove agency from individual actors and valorize structure over practice. Bourdieu criticizes any method that would attempt to remove agency and practice from our understanding of social structure. Similarly, a habitus is not a fixed or static system. Bourdieu asserts that distinctions between one habitus and another are not rigidly set, but have a shared and processual quality. Dispositions are multiple—we may, for example, apply one set of dispositions in our home life and another while at work—and changeable over time.

How does one come to or learn a particular habitus? Bourdieu describes this process as one of informal, unconscious learning rather than formal instruction. One learns to inhabit a habitus through practical means, such as using a particular space for a specific purpose, listening to music, cooking, drinking, wearing clothes, driving cars, celebrating holidays, and giving gifts. The habitus one occupies shapes the practices that one engages in. For Bourdieu, the notion of habitus reveals that while a person's behavior may be in part determined by formal social rules and mental ideas—uncovered and described by the social scientist—a significant determinant of behavior is hidden, implicit knowledge learned informally and embodied in specific social practices. Once internalized, habitus dispositions are taken for granted. Bourdieu uses the term **doxa** to refer to the taken-for-granted, unquestioned, unexamined ideas about social life that seem commonsensical and natural to the one possessing these dispositions.

Bourdieu's notion of habitus is not simply about a process of socialization or enculturation into a set of practices, but is also concerned with the power relations that exist between social classes, that is, with how social inequality is perpetrated and maintained. Habitus functions to distinguish social classes from each other. It is Bourdieu's unique version of ideology. Habitus contrasts the different sets of dispositions (social expectations, lifestyle choices, etc.) that exist between different classes. Class distinctions appear clearly in the complex of practices embedded in a particular habitus. One reason why this is so socially powerful, according to Bourdieu, is because class inequalities and the dominance of one class over another occur covertly. Rather than the application of overt force, symbolic power is harnessed to maintain class distinctions and the appearance of their naturalness. Money may have economic exchange value for food and other commodities, but the possession and use of it also have symbolic exchange value that marks one as wealthy and upper class or poor and lower class. Domination occurs, in part, because the exchange value system is itself controlled by the dominant class.

In order to explain the relation between habitus and social stratification more fully, Bourdieu borrows the economic term "capital," which he employs to refer not only to financial assets but also to other resources that confer status and reveal social class. Financial capital matters for the establishment of class distinctions, of course, but so does **cultural capital**, including educational level, linguistic competence, and other forms of capital that mark social class. Cultural capital is used to distinguish and maintain class distinctions and, by extension, social inequality.

Bourdieu also employs the category of **taste** to describe how distinctions between high and low culture are made and justified. In his own research, he found correlations between French aesthetic preferences for the arts on the one hand and "taste" preferences for such things as food and fashion on the other. He found that such tastes, like other forms of cultural capital, serve to demarcate class differences. Because taste marks distinctions between different levels of socioeconomic status and level of cultural refinement, it is also an ideological category. Thus, for Bourdieu, distinctions based on taste are part of the arsenal for differentiating social classes: "Taste classifies, and it classifies the classifier. Social subjects, classified by their classifications, distinguish themselves by the distinctions they make, between the beautiful and the ugly, the distinguished and the vulgar, in which their position in the objective classification is expressed or betrayed" (*Distinction*, p. 6).

There are numerous possibilities for employing Bourdieu's social theory in the field of academic religious studies. In particular, his approach draws our attention to the aspects of habitus that function to shape social behavior and power relations within a religion, and between a religious group and its larger social and cultural contexts. Religion, Bourdieu reminds us, is not simply about those beliefs and practices that are explicit and conscious within a religious tradition (e.g., a Roman Catholic view of sin and atonement, or the daily rituals performed by a Hindu). At least as important to a religious group are those more or less invisible dimensions of its habitus—doxa, tastes, and forms of cultural capital that operate within it to create cohesion and identity. Moreover, beyond their function within the group, these dimensions also may serve to determine the social location of its members within the larger class structure of a society. Consider, for example, correlations of taste, doxa, cultural capital, and social class among northeastern urban Episcopalians on the one hand and among midwestern rural Pentecostals on the other. Where does religion end and social class begin? Clearly, a religious habitus is never separate from the larger social structures and hierarchies of culture in which it is situated.

FURTHER READING
By Bourdieu

*An Outline of a Theory of Practice. Translated by Richard Nice. Cambridge: Cambridge University Press, 1977.

*Distinction: A Social Critique of the Judgment of Taste. Translated by Richard Nice. Cambridge: Harvard University Press, 1984.

The Logic of Practice. Translated by Richard Nice. Stanford: Stanford University Press, 1990.

The Field of Cultural Production: Essays on Art and Literature. Edited by Randal Johnson. Cambridge: Polity Press, 1993.

About Bourdieu

Akinnaso, F. Niyi. "Bourdieu and the Diviner: Knowledge and Symbolic Power in Yoruba Divination." In The Pursuit of Certainty: Religious and Cultural Formulations, edited by Wendy James. London and New York: Routledge, 1995.

Goodchild, Philip. "Job as Apologetic: The Role of the Audience." Religion 30 (2000): 149–67.

Heine, Steven. "Putting the 'Fox' Back in the 'Wild Fox Koan': The Intersection of Philosophical and Popular Religious Elements in the Ch'an/Zen Koan Tradition." Harvard Journal of Asiatic Studies 56 (1996): 257–317.

*Jenkins, Richard. Pierre Bourdieu. Rev. ed. London and New York: Routledge, 2002.

Lane, Jeremy F. Pierre Bourdieu: A Critical Introduction. London: Pluto Press, 2000.

Shusterman, Richard, ed. Bourdieu: A Critical Reader. Oxford: Blackwell Publishers, 1999.

Swartz, David. Culture and Power: The Sociology of Pierre Bourdieu. Chicago: University of Chicago Press, 1997.

JUDITH BUTLER

Key Concepts

- gender/sex
- performativity
- gender trouble
- paradox of subjection
- face of the enemy

Judith Butler (1956–) is Maxine Elliot Professor in the Departments of Rhetoric and Comparative Literature at the University of California, Berkeley. She received her Ph.D. in philosophy from Yale University in 1984. Butler understands her interest in philosophy as having derived in part from experiences as a child attending synagogue. "I came to ask certain questions about ethics and human life and violence within the context of a post-Holocaust Jewish education. A lot of my close textual analysis comes out of my understanding of what a reading of the Torah might be" ("Judith Butler 1.22.02," p. 9).

Butler is best known as a theorist of gender, identity, and power. Her most influential book to date, *Gender Trouble* (1990), makes the revolutionary argument that neither **gender** nor **sex** is natural nor are they categories of human identity. At the time, this was a major challenge to the then-common position among feminists that gender (masculinity and femininity) is culturally constructed, whereas sex (male and female) is natural and pre-given. In *Gender Trouble* and the subsequent *Bodies That Matter* (1993), Butler countered that "gender must . . . designate the very apparatus of production whereby the sexes themselves are established. As a result, gender is not to culture as sex is to nature; gender is also the discursive/cultural means by which 'sexed nature' or 'a natural sex' is produced and established as . . . prior to culture, a politically neutral surface on which culture acts" (*Gender Trouble*, p. 7). In other words, there is no male and female prior to cultural engenderings of those two categories of identity. We cannot think outside our culture, and "male" and "female" identities are as culturally determined as are "masculinity" and "femininity." That sexual identity is natural, that there are two sexes in nature, is a cultural idea.

Butler argues that these categories of identity take social and symbolic form in a culture through repeated action. Sexual identity is "**performative**." "There is no gender identity behind the expressions of gender ... identity is performatively constituted by the very 'expressions' that are said to be its results" (*Gender Trouble*, p. 25). Gender is not being but doing; it's not who you *are* but what you *do*. In other words, how you express your identity in word, action, dress, and manner determines gender.

Butler is critical of forms of feminism that assert "women" as a group with a distinct identity, set of political interests, form of social agency, and so on. In making such assertions, she contends, feminism risks reinforcing a binary conception of gender, thereby reducing the infinite possibilities of social identity for human beings to two categories, man and woman, defined in opposition to one another. Against this, Butler calls for performances that produce "**gender trouble**" within this social and symbolic order: drawing out the contradictions and excesses within oneself—the parts that do not "come together" into a simple, unified "whole" self—and acting out a multiplicity of gendered and sexual identities. Thus a multiplicity of gendered and sexual identities would be produced, troubling the binary oppositions that reduce woman to man's other and vice-versa, and opening up new forms of social agency and ways of being in the world.

In developing her theory of the performativity of gender and sex, Butler draws from Michel **FOUCAULT**'s understanding of power. Arguing against a reductionistic view of power as the dominant force of law, Foucault conceives of power as a "multiple and mobile field of force relations, wherein far-reaching, but never completely stable, effects of domination are produced" (*The History of Sexuality, Vol. 1: An Introduction*, p. 102). Power takes form within society through ceaseless struggles and renegotiations. It does not simply come down from on high but circulates through society. In the process, it materializes, takes a "terminal form," within a particular sociopolitical system of power/knowledge. Yet the "terminal forms" power takes are never entirely stable because they can never contain or totalize all actual and potential forces within it. Although they appear to us as terminal and fixed, they are in fact quite temporary and precarious. There are always points of resistance that cut across the social order and its stratifications of power and privilege, opening possibilities for subversion.

In *Gender Trouble* and later works, Butler develops Foucault's critical insights into the formation and subversion of terminal forms of power in relation to gender and sexual identity politics. Butler conceives of every social-symbolic order as a regulatory consolidation of power in the Foucauldian sense. Such an order is established and maintained by prohibitions and repeated performances of identities within that order. Yet, as Butler puts it, to be *constituted* within such a social-symbolic order is not to be *determined* by it. There is always the possibility of agency, of acting out within the system in ways that are subversive and transformative of it, because there are always aspects of oneself that are "socially impossible," that cannot be reduced to the order of things, that exceed any particular identity (such as gender identity and sexual identity) within that order, hence her interest in drag, cross-dressing, and other queer forms of gender trouble. Butler calls for performances, that is, expressions of identity that exploit those subversive dimensions, and thereby produce new possible ways of being in society.

In *The Psychic Life of Power*, Butler engages **FOUCAULT**, **FREUD**, **LACAN**, **ALTHUSSER**, and others to explore a related paradox of social-symbolic agency, which she describes as the "**paradox of subjection**." The paradox lies in the fact that subjectivity is founded on subjection. That is, in order to become an acting subject in a society, one must be subjected to its order (its language, laws, values, etc.). Recall Luce **IRIGARAY**'s description of the social-symbolic order of patriarchy as "a certain game" in which a woman finds herself "signed up without having begun to play" (*Speculum of the Other Woman*, p. 22). So it is, in fact, with all forms of subjectivity. One acts *within* a certain social-symbolic order, a certain "game" with certain rules to which and by which she is initially "subjected." Even if her actions are ultimately subversive of that order, her subjectivity is inaugurated through subjection to it. Thus Butler writes: "Subjection signifies the process of becoming subordinated by power as well as the process of becoming a subject" (*Psychic Life*, p. 2). She continues: "A power exerted on a subject, subjection is nevertheless a power assumed by the subject, an assumption that constitutes the instrument of that subject's becoming" (*Psychic Life*, p. 11). To have power is, paradoxically, to be subjected to power. "What does it mean" she asks, "that the subject, defended by some as the presupposition of agency, is also understood to be an *effect* of subjection?" (*Psychic Life*, p. 11). What it means, she argues, is that to be conditioned or formed by a certain terminal form of power is not to be determined by it. That is, a subject's agency, her own exercise of power, is not "tethered" to the conditions that formed her. The subject is, in one sense, an effect of power; through the same subject's own agency, power becomes the effect of the subject.

Butler has applied her theoretical interests in identity politics, subjectivity, and power to issues of ethics and violence in the war-torn aftermath of September 11, 2001. In particular, she focuses on media representations of the **face of the enemy**. How is it that America's enemies have been othered in such a way as to render them inhuman and their lives ungrievable, thereby turning us away from the reality of life as fragile and precarious? Exploring this problem in her essay "Precarious Life" (2003), Butler draws on Emmanuel **LEVINAS**'s concept of the face-to-face encounter as an ultimate ethical situation, a moment of obligation to the other, who pleads "do not kill." Media images reduce the face of the other to enemy (both as target and as victim of war) and thereby rule out the possibility of a genuine face-to-face encounter in the Levinasian sense. In these media representations, the "ultimate situation" of the face-to-face is foreclosed. How, Butler asks, has the face of the other been erased by these dehumanized faces, and how does one tell the stories of these lives in such as way as to recuperate the ethical possibility of opening oneself to them in obligation and grief?

To date, Butler's influence on religious studies has been concentrated at the intersection of religion, gender, and feminism. On the one hand, scholars are interested in how religious discourses, as part of larger social-symbolic orders, construct and constrict gender identities, as well as how they open up possibilities for subversion of identity (see Beal on gender and ethnic identity subversion in the Book of Esther and the related Jewish holiday of Purim in his *The Book of Hiding: Gender, Ethnicity, Annihilation, and Esther*).

Beyond appropriations of her early writing in *Gender Trouble* and *Bodies That Matter* on the creation and subversion of sexual identities, Butler's work on the paradox of subjection bears great possibilities for students of religion. In particular, how is it that religious beliefs, institutions, and practices serve the process of subjection—both as subjugation and empowerment—of the religious subject within a religious community or a religious tradition? How do the conditions that form the religious subject produce ambivalence within her psychic life? How do they work to form mechanisms of repression and desire? And what, in this context, is *religious* desire or longing?

Butler's work on identity as performative is also suggestive vis-à-vis the study of ritual. How, for example, do rituals, as highly regulated repeat performances, construct and constrict the identities of its performers (e.g., as priest, communicant, healer, shaman; unclean, clean, sacred, profane, etc.)? By the same token, how are rituals, as necessarily unstable "terminal forms" of power, open to subversion and therefore transformation by their acting subjects (e.g., a gay priest administering Holy Communion, a rock band replacing a church organist)? How do the various aspects of a religious subject always exceed her ritually prescribed identity in "socially impossible" and potentially subversive ways? How do ritual traditions immune themselves to such subversion, and how do they open themselves up to it?

Further Reading
By Butler

Gender Trouble: Feminism and the Subversion of Identity. New York and London: Routledge, 1990.
Bodies That Matter: On the Discursive Limits of "Sex." New York and London: Routledge, 1993.
The Psychic Life of Power: Theories of Subjection. Stanford: Stanford University Press, 1997.

"Judith Butler 1.22.02." Interview. Common Sense Winter 2002: 9–12.

"Precarious Life." Meeting of the Consortium of Humanities Centers and Institutes. Harvard University. Cambridge. March 15, 2003.

About Butler

Beal, Timothy K. "Subversive Excesses." In *The Book of Hiding: Gender, Ethnicity, Annihilation, and Esther*. London and New York: Routledge, 1997.

*Boyarin, Daniel. "Gender." In *Critical Terms for Religious Study*, edited by Mark C. Taylor. Chicago: University of Chicago Press, 1998.

Fulkerson, Mary McClintock. "Gender—Being It or Doing It? The Church, Homosexuality, and the Politics of Identity." *Que(e)rying Religion: A Critical Anthology*, edited by David Comstock and Susan E. Henking. New York: Continuum, 1997.

Gottschall, M. "The Ethical Implications of the Deconstruction of Gender." *Journal of the American Academy of Religion* 70 (2002): 279–99.

Jantzen, Grace M. "What's the Difference? Knowledge and Gender in (Post) Modern Philosophy of Religion." *Religious Studies* 32 (1996): 431–48.

Parsons, Susan F. "The Boundaries of Desire: A Consideration of Judith Butler and Carter Heyward." *Feminist Theology* 23 (2000): 90–104.

HÉLÈNE CIXOUS

Key Concepts

- Jewoman
- *écriture féminine*
- the Hebrew Bible and the unconscious

Hélène Cixous (1937–) is professor of literature at the University of Paris VIII, an experimental university that she helped to found in 1968, and where she established a doctoral program in women's studies, the first and only one in France. Her childhood, as she describes it, was simultaneously Mediterranean and Nordic. Raised in Oran, Algeria, her father's Jewish family had fled Spain for Morocco and spoke French, Spanish, and Arabic. Her Jewish mother and grandmother were German, and German was spoken in her home. She also learned Arabic and Hebrew from her father, who died in 1948. She learned English as a student in London in 1950, and moved to France in 1955 and became a student at Lycée Lakanal, a preparatory school for boys.

Given her life story, it comes as no surprise that she has always had a sense of homelessness and otherness wherever she found herself, without legitimate place, without "fatherland." Cixous captures this sense of homelessness and hybridity in her self-description as "**Jewoman**." "This is a thought, that we Jewomen have all the time, the thought of the good and bad luck, of chance, immigration, and exile" ("We Who Are Free," p. 204). Indeed, for Cixous, this groundless multiplicity of selves—this experience of fitting in anywhere and nowhere, without fatherland and without singular identity—becomes, in writing, the source of creativity. Writing allows her to create a "country of words," a home away from home. Indeed, for Cixous, it is precisely her sense of dislocation and perpetual immigration that, paradoxically, becomes the generative space of writing.

In an endorsement that has appeared on nearly every book by Cixous since the early 1990s, her longtime friend Jacques **DERRIDA** has called her the greatest contemporary writer in the French language. Part of what makes her writing so great, according to Derrida, is that she is a "poet-thinker, very much a poet and very much a thinking poet." Her writing is a kind of thinking about writing in which she follows her own creative process as it takes her into unfamiliar territories. "It's not a question of drawing the contours, *but what escapes the contour*, the secret movement, the breaking, the torment, the unexpected" ("Without End," p. 96). It is precisely this self-reflective—often autobiographical—thinking about writing, as she encounters the "unexpected" while pursuing "what escapes," that has made her such an important figure for scholars concerned with theory. If she "does" theory, it is toward a theory of writing.

Indeed, we might think of Cixous' writing as a kind of *poetics of deconstruction*. As it follows what escapes the main contours of thought, she watches those contours dissolve and new landscapes emerge. In this process, she and her readers become increasingly aware that the main contours have been keeping them from unknown worlds of possibility. Writing thus becomes a process of opening toward the mystery of the other. "The prisons precede me. When I have escaped them, I discover them: when they have cracked and split open beneath my feet" ("We Who Are Free," p. 203). In this respect, she does with her poetic writing what her contemporary Julia **KRISTEVA** looks for in her early semiotic analysis of literature, that is, a kind of revolutionary poetic language which can produce an "other" kind of subjectivity capable of opening new possibilities for social relations and community that are subversive of the dominant patriarchal, capitalistic social-symbolic order.

A key concept in Cixous' early writings, such as "The Laugh of the Medusa" (1975) and *The Newly Born Woman* (first published in French in 1975), is that of *écriture féminine*, or feminine/female writing. Such writing has its source not just in poststructuralist Barthesian theory, but in the embodied life experiences of women, and is closely related to a woman's speaking voice. The author of this kind of writing "signifies . . . with her body." Contrasted against the univocal, authoritative, disembodied voice of the father identified with the symbolic order of things, *écriture féminine* is multivocal, "pregnant with beginnings," subversive, and embodied. In this kind of writing, moreover, there is a bond not only between the text and the body that wrote it, but also between that body and its original bond with the mother. In the lyrical voice of *écriture féminine*, one can hear the mother's song as heard by the child before she could speak, that first voice which all women preserve in their own living voices.

Although Cixous does not address religion specifically, her writing does often draw from religious scriptures, especially stories from the **Hebrew Bible** (e.g., "Coming to Writing" and *Veils*). In *Three Steps on the Ladder of Writing* (1993), she speaks directly about her understanding of the Hebrew Bible and why she so often returns to it for poetic inspiration. In these stories, she finds a wonderful crudeness, a shameless presentation of raw humanity that locates the Bible more with the **unconscious** than with the states of repression that normally rule our conscious social lives. "The Bible's Moses," for example, "cuts himself shaving. He is afraid, he is a liar. He does many a thing under the table before being Up There with the other Tables. This is what the oneiric world of the Bible makes apparent to us. The light that bathes the Bible has the same crude and shameless color as the light that reigns over the unconscious" (p. 67).

Further Reading

By Cixous

*The Hélène Cixous Reader. Edited by Susan Sellers. New York and London: Routledge, 1994.

"We Who Are We, Are We Free?" Oxford Amnesty Lecture, February 1992. Translated by Chris Miller. *Critical Inquiry* 19 (1993): 201–19.

"Without End No State of Drawingness No, Rather: The Executioner's Taking Off." Translated by Catherine A.F. MacGillivray. *New Literary History* 24 (1993): 91–103.

(with Catherine Clément) *The Newly Born Woman*. Translated by Betsy Wing. Minnesota: University of Minnesota Press, 1986.

"Coming to Writing" and Other Essays. Edited by Deborah Jenson and translated by Sarah Cornell, Deborah Jenson, Ann Liddle, and Susan Sellers. Cambridge: Harvard University Press, 1991.

"The Laugh of the Medusa." Translated by Keith Cohen and Paula Cohen of a revised version of "Le rire de la Méduse." *Signs* 1 (1975): 875–93.

(with Jacques Derrida) *Veils*. Translated by Geoffrey Bennington. Stanford: Stanford University Press, 2001.

Three Steps on the Ladder of Writing. Translated by Sarah Cornell and Susan Sellers. New York: Columbia University Press, 1993.

Rootprints: Memory and Life Writing. Edited by Hélène Cixous and Mireille Calle-Gruber and translated by Eric Prenowitz. London and New York: Routledge, 1997.

About Cixous

Armour, Ellen T. "Recent French Feminist Works." *Religious Studies Review* 17 (1991): 205–08.

Beal, Timothy K. "Subversive Excesses." In *The Book of Hiding: Gender, Ethnicity, Annihilation, and Esther*. London and New York: Routledge, 1997.

Carrera, Elena. "The Fertile Mystical Maze: From Derrida's Dry Theological Gorge to Cixous's Dialogic Disgorging." In *Trajectories of Mysticism in Theory and Literature*, edited by Philip Leonard. New York: St. Martin's Press, 2000.

*Joy, Morny, Kathleen O'Grady, and Judith L. Poxon, eds. *French Feminists on Religion: A Reader*. London and New York: Routledge, 2002.

*Moi, Toril. *Sexual/Textual Politics: Feminist Literary Theory*. London and New York: Routledge, 1985.

Upton, Lee. "Coming to God." *Denver Quarterly* 27 (1993): 83–94.

GILLES DELEUZE
AND FÉLIX GUATTARI

Key Concepts

- rhizome
- aborescence
- schizoanalysis
- desire as flow
- desiring machines
- body without organs
- deterritorialization

Gilles Deleuze (1925–95) was a philosopher. He was born in France in 1925 and, after a long illness, committed suicide in 1995. He studied at the Sorbonne under Georges Canguilhem and Jean Hyppolite. He later taught philosophy at the Sorbonne, the University of Lyon, and, at the invitation of Michel **FOUCAULT**, at the experimental University of Paris VIII. He retired in 1987. Deleuze was a prolific writer, penning individual monographs on both philosophy and literature, including studies of Hume, Bergson, Spinoza, Nietzsche, Proust, Atrtaud, and Lewis Carroll; critiques of Kantian and Platonic thought; and considerations of such issues as representation, linguistic meaning, subjectivity, and difference.

Félix Guattari (1930–92) was a noted psychoanalyst and political activist. He was born in France in 1930 and died in 1992 of a heart attack. He embraced both radical psychotherapy ("anti-psychiatry") and Marxist politics, though he became disillusioned with the French Communist Party after the May 1968 Paris strikes. He was a psychoanalyst at the Clinique de la Borde from 1953 until his death and was known for his use of alternative psychoanalytic therapies. Guattari was also closely associated with Lacanian psychoanalytic theory. He received training from Jacques **LACAN** and was in analysis with him from 1962 to 1969. He later came to critique at least some aspects of Lacanian analysis. Guattari individually published essays and two books on psychoanalytic theory. In addition to his work with Deleuze, he collaborated with other Marxist thinkers and psychoanalysts.

Deleuze and Guattari met in 1969 and started working together soon after. Their collaborations included four books that are especially noteworthy for their dual critiques of Marxist and Freudian thought. The writings we will deal with here are the two volumes of *Capitalism and Schizophrenia: Anti-Oedipus* (first published in French in 1972) and *A Thousand Plateaus* (first published in French in 1980). In these twin volumes, Deleuze and Guattari attempt to destabilize essentialism and grand theories—especially those of Marx, Freud, and structuralism. Deleuze and Guattari leave us with a very rich conceptual palette replete with many neologisms, only a small part of which we can discuss here.

Despite the tendency among many to associate Deleuze and Guattari with "postmodernism," they did not themselves see their intellectual project in this light. Guattari, for instance, repudiated postmodernism as "nothing but the last gasp of modernism; nothing, that is, but a reaction to and, in a certain way, a mirror of the formalist abuses and reductions of modernism from which, in the end, it is no different" ("The Postmodern Impasse," p. 109). The postmodern label notwithstanding, Deleuze and Guattari crafted a view of the world critical of grand narratives (see **LYOTARD**), foundational thought, and essences. Resisting those tendencies of modern thought, their texts describe ways of seeing and understanding multiplicities both of individual subjects and larger institutional entities. It is to the end of destabilizing what they refer to as fascist ways of acting in the world that they arm themselves with a battery of neologisms that force us to think and conceptualize outside established, hegemonic, and naturalized modes of modern commonsense.

Because Deleuze and Guattari seek multiplicity in their writing style, it is difficult to derive a clear and linear outline of their ideas. Any attempt to do so runs counter to their own resistance to such modernist ways of thinking. Many of the neologisms they employ are more suggestive than definitive, but we can point out some of the recurring themes and concepts with which Deleuze and Guattari are concerned. In general, Deleuze and Guattari engage in insistent critiques of modern ideas concerning the primacy of hierarchy, truth, meaning, subjectivity, and representation. For instance, Deleuze and Guattari attack the notion that there exist individual subjects who can gain knowledge of the truth and then transmit (represent) that truth transparently to others.

One notion that underscores their attempt to derail modernist, linear thinking is their use of the metaphor of the **rhizome**, an idea taken up at the beginning of *A Thousand Plateaus*. A rhizome is a botanical term referring to a horizontal stem (like crabgrass), usually underground, that sends out roots and shoots from multiple nodes. It is not possible to locate a rhizome's source root. Rhizomatic thinking contrasts with **arborescent** (treelike) thinking that develops from root to trunk to branch to leaf. Aborescent modes of thought, according to Deleuze and Guattari, are especially characteristic of the grand narratives of modernist, capitalist thought. Deleuze and Guattari protest: "We're tired of trees. We should stop believing in trees, roots, and radicals. They've made us suffer too much. All of arborescent culture is founded on them, from biology to linguistics. Nothing is beautiful or loving or political aside from underground stems and aerial roots, adventitious growths and rhizomes" (*A Thousand Plateaus*, p. 15). According to Deleuze and Guattari, the arborescent mode, which has dominated Western thought, is hegemonic in that it naturalizes hierarchic orders and gives priority to narratives of origin. Rhizomatic thought suggests a non-hierarchy of multiple narratives without origin or central root to serve as the source.

To disrupt arborescent thought is to question modern conceptions of human subjectivity. Arborescence sees the world in terms of freely choosing, autonomous, individual entities—like free-standing trees. In such a mode of thinking, subject/object dichotomies abound. Deleuze and Guattari insist that we need to subvert this order through rhizomatic thinking that looks at the world in terms of relationship and heterogeneity. Deleuze and Guattari provide the example of the wasp and the orchid. Rather than describing each in the arborescent, hierarchical terminology of separate entities with distinct essences, Deleuze and Guattari require us to look at the interconnections, the points where the notion of individuality and essence break down. Thus they state that "[w]asp and orchid, as heterogeneous elements, form a rhizome" (*A Thousand Plateaus*, p. 10). The point is this: from a rhizomatic perspective, the wasp and orchid are implicated with each other. The wasp is part of the orchid's reproductive process by transmitting pollen to it, and the orchid provides food for the wasp. They form not a system of individual entities or nodes, but an interconnected, transitory, rhizome where the boundary of wasp and orchid are blurred. To understand this process we need to think not in terms of individual entities, but rather in terms of "a becoming-wasp of the orchid and a becoming-orchid of the wasp" (*A Thousand Plateaus*, p. 10).

The rhizome metaphor is a critique of totalizing processes, systems that attempt to explain all things within one interpretive framework or hierarchical master code. To this critical end, they mount a blistering critique of the Freudian and Marxist master narratives that ultimately limit the complexity of reality with their *transcendent* interpretations of human subjectivity and history. They oppose these dominant, transcendent modes of interpretation with an *immanent* mode of interpretation that acknowledges and prizes complexities. According to Deleuze and Guattari, fascist oppression is the inevitable result of transcendent interpretations.

The first volume of *Capitalism and Schizophrenia*, *Anti-Oedipus*, takes up the political nature of desire. Deleuze and Guattari's criticism of psychoanalysis is made under the banner of "**schizoanalysis**," a rhizomatic alternative to the arborescent thinking of psychoanalysis. In their schizoanalytic critique of Freud, Deleuze and Guattari refute Freud's negative notion of desire as lack that is explained through the Oedipus complex. For Freud, the Oedipus complex transcends time and place and is a natural human disposition that is inescapable. For Deleuze and Guattari, this perspective is repressive because it subjects everyone to the same transcendent structure (mother-father-child). Rather than viewing the unconscious as characterized by desire and its lack, Deleuze and Guattari see the unconscious as productive of desire and hence in need of repressive control by the capitalist state. In analysis, the immanent interpretation of individuals is recast into the transcendent interpretation of Freudian desire, the family triangle. The individual is thereby subjected to the repression and restraint of the psychoanalytic interpretative framework, and the patient is subjected to the interpretation of the powerful and authoritative analyst.

Libidinal impulses are instead to be understood as *desire producing* and therefore potentially disruptive of a capitalist state, which wants to control desire and cast it in negative terms. Similarly, culture, language, and other symbolic systems are also repressive because they subject people to their rules and codes. In contrast to the symbolic is the imaginary, and they refer to schizophrenia as exemplary of this mode. The Oedipal is symbolic; the presymbolic is pre-Oedipal and thus prior to the hierarchy and repression of families (see also **LACAN**).

Schizoanalysis is a critique of psychoanalysis—an example of arborescent thinking—especially its conceptions of unconscious desire and the Oedipus complex. In traditional psychoanalysis, which is a transcendent mode of interpreting human subjects, negative Oedipal desire precedes any particular patient's narrative. That is, the interpretation of the reported narrative is known in advance by the analyst. The outcome of analysis is predetermined. The only thing the analyst will find is Oedipal conflict. In turn, as a means of control, desire is directed toward Oedipal prohibitions through this transcendent interpretation. "The law tells us: You will not marry your mother and you will not kill your father. And we docile subjects say to ourselves: so *that*'s what I wanted!" (*Anti-Oedipus*, p. 114).

Deleuze and Guattari refer to schizophrenics as metaphorically exemplary of their arguments because of the fragmented nature of their subjectivity and desire that allows them to stand outside the repressions placed on the "normal": "But such a man produces himself as a free man, irresponsible, solitary, and joyous, finally able to say and do something simple in his own name, without asking permission; a desire lacking nothing, a flux that overcomes barriers and codes, a name that no longer designates any ego whatever. He has simply ceased being afraid of becoming mad. He experiences and lives himself as the sublime sickness that will no longer affect him" (*Anti-Oedipus*, p. 131).

Desire, as conceived of in psychoanalysis, is something to be repressed and contained. Seeking to liberate desire from this negative charge, Deleuze and Guattari develop an understanding of **desire as a flow** of libido that exists prior to any representation of desire in psychoanalysis. Desire becomes "territorialized" through political and ideological structures like family, religion, school, medicine, nation, sports, and media. From an arborescent perspective, these structures subject the self–conceived of as autonomous—to their totalizing discourses. Deleuze and Guattari want to open possibilities for desire to flow in multiple ways and directions at once, regardless of socially sanctioned boundaries that otherwise seek to control that flow. Again, the schizophrenic stands for this possibility.

Deleuze and Guattari conceive of human beings as "**desiring-machines.**" This refers, in part, to the idea that desire stems from a moment prior to structure and representation. Bodies are "desiring-machines," in which such things as ideas, feelings, and desires flow in and out of one body-machine and into and out of other desiring-machines. Desire is like a machine in that both are productive. For instance, a furnace-machine produces heat; desire produces libidinal energy. The idea of machine also subverts traditional views of subjectivity.

A desiring-machine is connected to a "**body without organs**" (often abbreviated BwO), a term borrowed from avant-garde playwright Antonin Artaud (1896–1948). This concept denies the idea that the person is to be found inside the body, composed of autonomous, self-sustaining, and organized internal forms. Instead, BwO suggests that the person-body is interconnected, exterior, open, multiple, fragmented, provisional, and interpenetrated by other entities. In their words: "There is no such thing as either man or nature now, only a process that produces the one within the other and couples the machines together. Producing-machines, desiring-machines everywhere, schizophrenic machines, all of species life: the self and the non-self, outside and inside, no longer have any meaning whatsoever" (*Anti-Oedipus*, p. 2).

Schizoanalysis seeks "**deterritorialization,**" a space where desire is liberated from the constraints of the psychoanalytic. The deterritorialized is the space (both spatial and psychic) occupied by the metaphorical body without organs. This contrasts with territorialization and reterritorialization—the attempts to totalize, to structure hierarchically, to contain—through institutions such as religion, family, and school. For Deleuze and Guattari, to (re)territorialize is to try to contain and place boundaries around desire, to repress it. The deterritorialized is fragmented, multiple, uncontained. In such a space, boundaries are fluid, selves transform, desire flows in multiple directions.

There are significant implications for religious studies in the work of Deleuze and Guattari, although their ideas are not yet widely utilized by religion scholars. In the first place, traditional religions are typically arborescent systems. They assert hierarchy, claim transcendent foundations, repress the flow of desire, and construct individual subjects in need of salvation or some other form of transformation. Usually it is the internal world of the individual that requires transformation, and the Western propensity to think of religion in terms of belief—an interior commitment—is an example of the arborescent idea that the self or soul is the subject's center. Schizoanalysis runs counter to these views, calling into question all of these assumptions and interrogating the ramifications, ideological and otherwise, for holding them. For Deleuze and Guattari, what we refer to as the "self" is merely the locus from which machinic assemblages converge and interact, creating impermanent, dynamic connections that are in constant flux. There is no individual or fundamental unity that is the core (soul) of the person, there is only fragmentation. The schizophrenic is a metaphor for this way of being in the world. Human subjectivity must be understood in terms of relationship and interconnectedness.

Further Reading

By Deleuze and Guattari

*A Thousand Plateaus: Capitalism and Schizophrenia. Translated by Brian Massumi. Minneapolis: University of Minnesota Press, 1987.

*Anti-Oedipus: Capitalism and Schizophrenia. Translated by Robert Hurley, Mark Seem, and Helen R. Lane. Minneapolis: University of Minnesota Press, 1983.

Guattari, Félix. "The Postmodern Impasse." In The Guattari Reader, edited by Gary Genosko. Oxford: Blackwell, 1996.

About Deleuze and/or Guattari

*Bogue, Ronald. Deleuze and Guattari. London and New York, Routledge, 1989.

Bryden, Mary, ed. Deleuze and Religion. London and New York: Routledge, 2001.

Buchanan, Ian and Claire Colebrook, eds. Deleuze and Feminist Theory. Edinburgh: Edinburgh University Press, 2000.

Glass, Newman Robert. "Splits and Gaps in Buddhism and Postmodern Theology." Journal of the American Academy of Religion 63 (1995): 303–19.

Goodchild, Philip. "A Theological Passion for Deleuze." Theology 99 (1996): 357–65.

Marrati, Paola. "'The Catholicism of Cinema': Gilles Deleuze on Image and Belief." In Religion and Media, edited by Hent de Vries and Samuel Weber. Stanford: Stanford University Press, 2001.

Massumi, Brian. User's Guide to Capitalism and Schizophrenia: Deviations from Deleuze and Guattari. Cambridge: MIT Press, 1992.

Stivale, Charles. The Two-Fold Thought of Deleuze and Guattari: Intersections and Animations. New York: Guilford Press, 1998.

Wyschogrod, Edith. Saints and Postmodernism: Revisioning Moral Philosophy. Chicago: University of Chicago Press, 1990.

JACQUES DERRIDA

Key Concepts

- deconstruction
- messianism
- globalatinization
- indemnification
- religion as immune system
- religion and auto-immune disorder

Jacques Derrida (1930–) was born to a middle-class Jewish family in the Algerian suburb El-Biar. At ten years old, when the war came to Algeria, he and the other Jews were expelled from the public school system and later (with the arrival of the Allied forces) enrolled in a Jewish school. He moved to France at nineteen years old where he began studies at the Grandes Ecole preparatory program and studied phenomenology with Emmanuel **LEVINAS**. He has taught at the Ecole Normale Supérieure and the École des Hautes Études in Paris and also holds teaching posts at several American universities, including Johns Hopkins University, New York University, and the University of California at Irvine. Throughout his career, he has demonstrated a strong commitment to public education, especially through his work with the Research Group on the Teaching of Philosophy, which advocates making philosophy a fundamental discipline in secondary school curriculum.

It would be impossible to summarize Derrida's work to date, even if we were to limit ourselves to his most influential contributions to philosophy, religion, linguistics, literary theory, and cultural studies. Yet there is a certain orientation that is consistent throughout his many texts. We might describe it as a kind of close reading that raises questions about "what is implicit in the accumulated reserve" ("An Interview with Derrrida," p. 108). Through relentlessly vigilant attention to the texts and discourses in which the fundamentals of Western thought are articulated, he works to reveal the uncertainties, instabilities, and impasses implicit in our intellectual traditions, moving us to the edges of knowing, at which point "what once seemed assured is now revealed in its precariousness" ("An Interview with Derrrida," p. 110). This is not, as his critics allege, out of some nihilistic contempt for all things Western or masturbatory fascination with groundless intellectual free play, but in order to destabilize assumptions enough to open spaces for continued reflection and the possibility of innovation and creative thinking. He treats Western intellectual tradition as a living discourse and works to keep our intellectual disciplines and educational institutions from ossifying.

This is the proper context in which to understand the term **deconstruction**, a concept that has too often been misunderstood by Derrida's readers, who do not always read him as well as he reads others. He first used it in *Of Grammatology* (first published in French in 1967; translated and introduced in English by Gayatri **SPIVAK**) while trying to translate Heidegger's term *Destruktion*, which in French carried the sense of annihilation or demolition as well as destructuration. At the time "deconstruction" was used very little in French and its primary sense was mechanical, referring to the process of disassembly in order to understand parts in relation to the whole. For Derrida, deconstruction was conceived not as a negative operation aimed only at tearing down, but rather as a kind of close analysis that seeks "to understand how an 'ensemble' was constituted and to reconstruct it to this end" ("Letter to a Japanese Friend," p. 4). It is in the process of reading closely, with an eye for how an idea is constructed, that one also comes to see the points of potential rupture, the cracks and other points of instability within the structure. It is in the process of close reading that one sees deconstruction happening. "Deconstruction takes place, it is an event that does not await the deliberation, consciousness or organization . . . It deconstructs it-self" ("Letter to a Japanese Friend," p. 5). That is, it *loses its construction*. Deconstruction happens. It is a matter of reading closely enough to see it happening within systems that we might otherwise assume to be stable—indeed, systems that we *depend* on being stable.

Deconstruction, then, is what happens when one works one's way through a certain logic of thinking in such a way as to reveal what that logic cannot admit, what it must exclude, the unthinkable, "the singularity that threatens generality . . . the anomalies that circulate within and open up the system" (Sherwood, "Derrida," p. 71). As one of Derrida's early translators put it, "the deconstructive reading does not point out the flaws or weaknesses or stupidities of an author, but the *necessity* with which what he *does* see is systematically related to what he does *not* see" (Johnson, "Translator's Introduction," *Dissemination*, p. xv).

Throughout his career, Derrida has been criticized for writing texts that are too difficult for many readers to understand. He defends his texts against such criticisms by pointing out why they are so difficult—namely, because they are fundamentally concerned with questioning precisely those things we think we understand. "No one gets angry with a mathematician or with a doctor he doesn't understand at all, or with someone who speaks a foreign language, but when somebody touches your own language. . . ." ("An Interview with Derrrida," p. 107).

Derrida first emerged as a major influence on philosophy and literary studies in 1967, with the simultaneous publication in French of three books: *Speech and Phenomena*, a treatise on Husserl's phenomenology; *Of Grammatology*, a critique of the way Western theories of language and communication have privileged speech over writing; and *Writing and Difference*, a collection of essays (some written as early as 1959) offering close readings of major contemporary figures including **SAUSSURE**, Lévi-Strauss, **LEVINAS**, and **BATAILLE**). Five years later, in 1972, he published three more: *Dissemination*, also on writing, with close readings of Plato, Mallarmé, and Sollers; *Positions*, a collection of interviews with him; and *Margins of Philosophy*, a series of close readings of philosophical texts, written at the margins of philosophical thought and in the margins of the texts themselves.

A year before his first book blitz in 1967, Derrida gave a lecture at Johns Hopkins University titled "Structure, Sign, and Play in the Discourse of the Human Sciences" (later published in *Writing and Difference*). More than any other, it is this essay that led to widespread association of him with "post-structuralism," a term invented not by Derrida but by American literary scholars who were appropriating his theories in their own research. A brief synopsis of this now classic essay provides a helpful way into Derrida's early thought, which remains highly influential to this day.

Derrida presents this essay in the aftermath of the intellectual revolution of structuralism, a linguistic turn in the history of Western thought, which he sees as a transformative moment, a destabilizing of inherited understandings about the trustworthy stability of language and meaning. He describes this complex transformation as the "moment when language invaded the universal problematic, the moment when, in the absence of a center or origin, everything became discourse . . . that is to say, a system in which the central signified, the original transcendental signified, is never absolutely present outside a system of differences" ("Structure, Sign, and Play," p. 280). Here he is referring to the linguistic turn of structuralism inaugurated by **SAUSSURE**. This absence of a structural center, foundation stone, or ordering principal ("God," "Being," or some other "transcendental signified") to language that would guarantee meaning and coherence within its system of signification "extends the domain and the play of signification infinitely" (p. 280). Here Derrida is not simply undermining Saussurean structuralism in the name of an infinite and unstable play of meaning; rather he is calling attention to the radical implication of structuralism, namely that *there is nothing outside language* to control, limit, or direct the play of signification. Signs are not inherently stable, so neither is meaning. Ultimate "undecidability" pervades all language.

Derrida then considers what our options are in the wake of the crisis in meaning he has just described. He identifies two responses, two "interpretations of interpretation." On the one hand, there is a melancholic, remorseful nostalgia for origins, a longing for "archaic and natural innocence" that "seeks to decipher, dreams of deciphering a truth or an origin which escapes play . . . and which lives the necessity of interpretation as an exile" (p. 292). Derrida sees Lévi-Strauss's search for the foundational elements of myth as an example of this mode of interpretation (another example can be found in Mircea Eliade's interpretation of cosmic religion as set against the profane homogeneity of modern society). On the other hand, there is the exuberant affirmation of play in a world without center or ground or security, as exemplified by **NIETZSCHE**. Both are responses to the modern Western experience of being ungrounded and dislocated. While one aches with nostalgia for that which is forever lost, the other gets lost in limitless, homeless play.

Derrida does not imagine that his articulation of the structuralist catastrophe itself is any great revelation; nor is his delineation of these two ways of responding to that catastrophe. In this essay, the real revelation—of some common ground in this new groundless situation—is yet to come. The catastrophic ungrounding of Western thought opens the world, as we know it and as we assumed it has always been known, to something radically other, proclaiming itself coming but not yet come. Like the scrolls seen but never read by John in the book of Revelation, the question here is revealed as awaiting revelation.

The sense of apocalyptic expectation we see at the end of this early essay—an expectation of something completely unknown and yet to be revealed—pervades much of Derrida's work. It appears most prominently, perhaps, in his discussions of **messianism** (especially in *Specters of Marx*), by which he refers to a kind of undeterminable, open-ended orientation toward that which is unknown and yet to come, the "other" that cannot be anticipated. In this respect, Derrida's messianism is "deserted" of its specific religious content. It is the "messianic in general, as a thinking of the other and of the event to come" (*Specters of Marx*, p. 59) without any particular content (e.g., the second coming of Christ, the end of the world in fire and blood, etc.). Thus he describes it as "messianism without religion, even a messianic without messianism" (*Specters of Marx*, p. 59; also p. 65; and Caputo, *Prayers and Tears*, pp. 128–30). Here, then, as elsewhere, Derrida takes a traditional form of theological discourse—apocalypticism and messianic expectation—and transforms it by emptying it of all religiously specific content. And so the much celebrated and highly exaggerated death of Marxism with the collapse of the Soviet Union becomes the occasion for a rebirth of **MARX**. Likewise, the death of religion or "God" becomes occasion for rebirth of the religious or the coming of an unknowable wholly other.

Since the mid-1990s, Derrida has increasingly been involved in conversations with philosophers around specific theoretical questions concerning religion. In 2002, he participated in a major series of programs and events focused on his work in relation to biblical studies at the annual meeting of the American Academy of Religion in Toronto (see Sherwood and Hart, *Other Testaments*, and Sherwood, *Derrida's Bible*). In 1997 and 1999, he participated in the biannual Religion and Postmodernism conferences at Villanova University (see, e.g., Caputo et al., *Questioning God*). Earlier, in 1994, he worked with Gianni Vattimo to organize a symposium of continental philosophers (including Hans-Georg **GADAMER**) in Capri, Italy, to address the subject of religion, especially as it relates to new realities of globalization (see Derrida and Vattimo, *Religion*).

Derrida's essay for the meeting at Capri, "Faith and Knowledge," written in fifty-two numbered paragraphs (recalling, perhaps, the fifty-two weekly readings in the Christian Lectionary of biblical lessons) is his most direct attempt to theorize "religion" and to understand the significance, at the turn of the twenty-first century, of what is often called "the return of the religious" in our so-called postmodern, post-Enlightenment world of global capitalism and transnational exchange of ideas and capital.

Derrida insists, first and foremost, that we never forget that the very term "religion" is a Latin, indeed Christian, term and that the whole history of comparative religion is deeply influenced by Christian thought. When we speak about religion, "we are already speaking Latin," a point he reiterates throughout the essay. By "religion," moreover, he does not simply refer to a narrow term describing a set of beliefs, rituals, and institutions of the Christian church. For Derrida, Western religion has shaped nearly all aspects of Western culture, including its juridical and legal systems, its forms of government, its fundamental values and concepts of human nature, society, democracy, justice, and so on.

Derrida explores "religion" as it passes beyond its original Western, Christian context (having "been to Rome and taken a detour through the United States") to become a "universal" term—a process he describes as religion's "**globalatinization**" (French *mondialatinization*), a form of imperialism that is rapidly remaking all the particular cultures of the world (including their "religions") into its own image. As Derrida traces the globalatinization of religion, accelerated in recent decades by new media and communication technologies that are rapidly exposing every last nook and cranny of human cultural diversity for all to see, he traces the spreading imperialism of a whole Western economy of law and politics. For religion, he insists, is the soul of the European-Anglo-American imperial "tele-technoscientific" machine.

Within this discussion of the globalatinization of religion, Derrida is particularly interested in how "religion" maintains its Western (Christian, Latin) identity as it finds its way into other cultures. As it exposes itself to its cultural "others," how does it remain intact, uncontaminated, "pure"? In exploring this question, he adopts the language of indemnification and especially immunity. Tracing the term back to its earliest uses, Derrida argues that religion is at core about rejection. That is, religion is a resistive response to the invasion of otherness, a rejection of anything foreign that might contaminate its wholeness and integrity. Thus religion is at heart about remaining *indemne*—"undamaged," "unscathed"—a word that is sometimes used in French to translate the German *heilig*, "holy" or "sacred." Religion's confessions and doctrines, for example, are forms of **indemnification** that prohibit and reject invasion by foreign ideas and practices, and its rituals of confession and communion are processes of restitution aimed at undoing damage and restoring purity.

The other language Derrida uses here is the biological language of immunity. Religion is an **immune system**: it works to keep the body of the community immune from contamination by foreign antibodies. Religion's beliefs, practices, and institutions work to immunize against outside threats of contamination— in other words, to protect the *indemne*, the undamaged wholeness/holiness of the social body. Derrida gives Islamist fundamentalism's rejection of "techno-economical modernity" as an example. Yet, as an immune system, religion is susceptible to its own self-destruction as well. That is, it can develop **auto-immune disorder**. Auto-immunity involves an organism's becoming immune to its own immune system, destroying its immunity, and opening itself to the other. Auto-immunity, then, is one way of thinking about how religion might *deconstruct itself*.

Derrida understands that this auto-immunity, this *rejection of religion's rejection* of otherness, is also at the heart of Western religious traditions. Certainly it is there in Jewish and Christian theologies of liberation, which see God as taking sides with the poor, the marginalized, the "stranger in your midst," and which call the faithful to do the same, thereby risking their own integrity and purity by opening themselves to the other. Indeed, in these Western religious traditions, it is an ethical imperative to open oneself to the stranger in the most radical way, in ways that even jeopardize one's own identity and security. Thus religion is in tension with itself, even in its core concepts of justice (Beal, "Specters of Moses"). On the one hand, as immune system, justice is conceived as prohibitive law and order. On the other hand, as auto-immunity, justice is conceived as self-transformative and self-risking openness to the other.

Further Reading

By Derrida

*"Villanova Roundtable." In *Deconstruction in a Nutshell: A Conversation with Jacques Derrida, with a Commentary by John D. Caputo*, edited by John D. Caputo. New York: Fordham University Press, 1997.

Acts of Religion. Edited by Gil Anidjar. New York and London: Routledge, 2002.

"Faith and Knowledge: The Two Sources of 'Religion' at the Limits of Reason Alone." Translated by Samuel Weber. In *Religion*, edited by Jacques Derrida and Gianni Vattimo. Stanford: Stanford University Press, 1998.

Of Grammatology. Translated by Gayatri Spivak. Baltimore: Johns Hopkins University Press, 1976; corrected edition 1998.

Dissemination. Translated by Barbara Johnson. Chicago: University of Chicago Press, 1981.

David, Catherine. "An Interview with Derrida." Translated by David Allison. In *Derrida and Difference*, edited by David Wood and Robert Bernasconi. Warwick: Parousia Press, 1985.

"On Forgiveness: A Roundtable Discussion with Jacques Derrida." Edited by Richard Kearney. In *Questioning God*, edited by John D. Caputo, Mark Dooley, and Michael J. Scanlon. Bloomington: Indiana University Press, 2001.

"Letter to a Japanese Friend." In *Derrida and Différance*, edited by David Wood and Robert Bernasconi. Warwick: Parousia Press, 1985.

Specters of Marx: The State of the Debt, the Work of Mourning and the New International. Translated by Peggy Kamuf. New York and London: Routledge, 1994.

Writing and Difference. Translated by Alan Bass. Chicago: University of Chicago Press, 1978.

About Derrida

Beal, Timothy K. "Specters of Moses." In *Imagining Biblical Worlds*, edited by David M. Gunn and Paula M. McNutt. New York: Continuum, 2003.

*Caputo, John D. *Prayers and Tears of Jacques Derrida: Religion without Religion*. Bloomington: Indiana University Press, 1997.

———. *Deconstruction in a Nutshell: A Conversation with Jacques Derrida, with a Commentary by John D. Caputo*. New York: Fordham University Press, 1997.

Handelman, Susan A. *The Slayers of Moses: The Emergence of Rabbinic Interpretation in Modern Literary Theory*. Albany: State University of New York Press, 1982.

Hart, Kevin, and Yvonne Sherwood, eds. *Derrida and Religion: Other Testaments*. New York and London: Routledge, 2004.

*Hart, Kevin. *The Trespass of the Sign: Deconstruction, Theology and Philosophy*. Cambridge: Cambridge University Press, 1985.

Linafelt, Tod. "The Undecidability of *brk* in the Prologue to Job and Beyond." *Biblical Interpretation* 4 (1995): 1–18.

Moore, Stephen D. *Mark and Luke in Poststructuralist Perspectives: Jesus Begins to Write*. New Haven: Yale University Press, 1992.

Schneidau, H. N. "The Word Against the Word: Derrida on Textuality." *Semeia* 23 (1982): 5–28.

Sherwood, Yvonne. "Derrida." In *Handbook of Postmodern Biblical Interpretation*, edited by A.K.M. Adam. St. Louis: Chalice, 2000.

Taylor, Mark C. *Tears*. Albany: State University of New York Press, 1990.

MICHEL FOUCAULT

Key Concepts

- archaeology of knowledge
- discourse
- genealogy
- power
- ethics of self

Michel Foucault (1926–84) was a French philosopher, social and intellectual historian, and cultural critic. He was born in Poitiers, the son of upper middle-class parents. He went to Paris after World War II and was admitted to the esteemed École normale supérieure in 1946, where he received degrees in philosophy (1948), psychology (1949), and his *agrégation* in philosophy (1952). Like many other French intellectuals in the 1940s and 1950s, Foucault became a member of the French Communist Party in 1950, but he left the party in 1953 after reading Nietzsche.

During the 1950s and early 1960s, Foucault held teaching positions at European universities while conducting research and writing his first widely influential books, including *Madness and Civilization* (published in French in 1961; submitted two years prior for his doctorate), *The Birth of the Clinic* (published in French in 1963), and *The Order of Things* (published in French in 1966), which became a best-seller in France and made Foucault a celebrity.

In response to the May 1968 strikes and student demonstrations, the French government opened the University of Paris VIII at Vincennes. Foucault, who had been working in Tunisia at the time of the demonstrations was named chair of its philosophy department. In 1970 Foucault was elected to the Collège de France, the country's most prestigious academic institution. This permanent appointment—as professor of the history of systems of thought—provided Foucault with a position in which he could devote nearly all his time to research and writing. His only teaching-related responsibility was to give an annual sequence of a dozen or so public lectures on his work.

During this period, Foucault became increasingly involved in social and political activism. His advocacy of prisoners' rights, for example, influenced his history of the prison system, *Discipline and Punish* (published in French in 1975). Around the same time, he turned his attention to sexuality, publishing the first of three volumes on the *History of Sexuality* in 1976. He completed the other two volumes shortly before his death due to AIDS-related complications in 1984.

Regardless of how one evaluates Foucault's scholarship, there is little doubt that the questions and issues he raised have permanently reshaped the humanities and social sciences. Foucault's scholarly output is impressive both for its quantity and for its breadth of interests and ideas. Among the topics he examined are madness, punishment, medicine, and sexuality. Religion also figures prominently— both implicitly and explicitly—throughout his work (see especially the collection of his writings on religion, *Religion and Culture* [1999]).

Foucault's work relentlessly challenges what counts as commonsense knowledge about human nature, history, and the world, as well as the social and political implications of such knowledge. Along the way, he questions the assumptions of such modernist masters as Freud and Marx whose ideas often underpin intellectual commonsense in twentieth-century France. More specifically, Foucault explores the parameters of what he calls the "human sciences," the academic field in which humanistic and social science discourses construct knowledge and subjectivity. He often writes on how various institutions (psychiatric clinics, prisons, schools, etc.) produce discourses that then constitute what can be known or practiced relative to that body of knowledge. People become disciplined subjects within these different discourses. In the process, he shows how knowledge and power are intimately connected. Therefore terms such as discourse, subjectivity, knowledge, and power are key to understanding Foucault's theories. These concepts, in turn, can be positioned within three areas that were central to Foucault's cultural analysis: (1) archaeology of knowledge, (2) genealogy of power, and (3) ethics. Underlying all three areas is a concern with the notion of the "subject" and the process of subjectivization, that is, the process by which a human subject is constituted (see also Judith **BUTLER** on the paradox of subjection, which she develops in relation to Foucault).

The **archaeology of knowledge** is the name Foucault gives (in a book by that title first published in French in 1969) to his method of intellectual inquiry. For Foucault, archaeology refers to a historical analysis that seeks to uncover **discourses** operating within systems of meaning. His concern is not with uncovering historical "truth," but rather with understanding how discursive formations—for example, medical discourse or discourse on sexuality—come to be seen as natural and self-evident, accurately representing a world of knowledge. Influenced by structuralism, Foucault sought to uncover structures and rules embedded in discourse through which knowledge is constructed and implemented. Discursive knowledge regulates, *inter alia*, what can be said and done, what constitutes right and wrong, and what counts for knowledge in the first place. In short, discourse establishes and controls knowledge. Medical discourse thus establishes medical knowledge and related practices, including the doctor-patient relationship, divisions between physical and mental illness, the value of medical services, status hierarchies within the medical profession, and who can produce medical discourse itself. Significantly, Foucault's archaeological method regards discourses as both fluid and mutable, and systematic and stable. Medical discourse during the Renaissance bears no necessary similarity to contemporary medical discourse, yet each has a distinctive historical archive. It is these historical shifts that Foucault aims to uncover through the archaeology of knowledge. He examines discourses of madness, reason, and mental asylums in *Madness and Civilization* and discourses of medical practices and the medical "gaze" in *The Birth of the Clinic.*

During the 1970s, Foucault devoted his research to what he described as the genealogy of power, that is, a history of the meanings and effects of power, and how discourse and "technologies of power" are employed to discipline human behavior. The term **genealogy** is used by Foucault to refer to a mode of historical analysis that he developed in texts such as *Discipline and Punish* (1975) and *The History of Sexuality, Volume 1: An Introduction* (1976). The concept of genealogy, borrowed from Nietzsche, is explained by Foucault in his 1971 article, "Nietzsche, Genealogy, History."

Foucault's understanding of the nature of history is significant for the way in which it subverts the commonsense teleological view of history as a narrative of the causes and effects that produce human events and are thus traceable, in a linear and logically satisfying fashion, backward to origins. Foucault also sees history as narrative, but one that is fragmented, nonlinear, discontinuous, and without the certitude of cause and effect. Foucault refers to this form of historical analysis as genealogy and describes it thus: "Genealogy is gray, meticulous and patiently documentary. It operates on a field of tangled and confused parchments, on documents that have been scratched over and recopied many times" ("Nietzsche, Genealogy, History," p. 139). For Foucault, history is textual and conveys a narrative that is ambiguous and conflicting. History bears the marks of repeated emendations—additions, deletions, embellishments, and other textual tinkering that makes it impossible to follow a cause-and-effect lineage back to an origin. For Foucault, any origin has long become obscured and unrecoverable. Historical truth suffers a similar fate, though truth claims are still made and are difficult to controvert. Foucault, following Nietzsche, sees truth as error: "Truth is undoubtedly the sort of error that cannot be refuted because it was hardened into an unalterable form in the long baking process of history" ("Nietzsche, Genealogy, History," p. 144).

Genealogy as a method underscores the interpretive nature of any narration of the past (see also Hayden **WHITE**). Indeed, the historical past is always and inevitably read through contemporary interests and concerns. Objectivity is questioned in favor of acknowledging the historian's political and ideological investment in the narrative being told. Even if historical truth exists, historians have no particular or privileged access to it. Foucault is most interested, then, in understanding historical documents as discourses of knowledge that highlight some perspectives while suppressing others. Foucault wants to reread the past and narrate that story from other perspectives. This genealogical approach runs counter to an idea of history as relating the "truth" of past events—of telling what "actually" happened. Rather than chasing after some ephemeral grand narrative that attempts to silence the discontinuities, Foucault seeks to interpret the past in ways that highlight the ambiguity, fragmentation, and struggle that necessarily accompany any historical analysis. For Foucault, if the concept of historical origin must be invoked, then it also must be acknowledged that there are multiple origins for any historical trajectory. History as one unified story gives way to a multiplicity of narratives about the past. Thus we begin to see history not in terms of a static and fixed past but as a continually changing narrative process.

Foucault applies his genealogical analysis to the history of **power**, exploring how power operates to produce particular kinds of subjects. For Foucault, power is not some monolithic force that appears in the same guises throughout all times and places. Instead, power has a genealogical history and is understood differently depending on place, location, and theoretical perspective. For instance, a Marxist view of power as that force wielded by governments, corporations, and others who control the economic means of production is very different from a feminist view of patriarchal power. Similarly, Foucault sees power as having a history that includes instances of both oppressive power and power as resistance to oppression. Foucault argues in "The Subject and Power" (1982) that the concept of power must always include the possibility of resistance to power. Power, therefore, is always a relationship, one that creates subjects. But power relationships can be resisted, which means that we can oppose the subject positions that discourses and material practices attempt to impose on us. For Foucault, power is capillary, flowing throughout the social body and not simply emanating from on high.

Genealogical inquiry is used by Foucault to further explicate ways in which power is implicated in how subjects and subjectivity are constructed. As Foucault noted in a 1980 lecture at Dartmouth College, "I have tried to get out from the philosophy of the subject through a genealogy of this subject, by studying the constitution of the subject across history which has led us up to the modern concept of the self. This has not always been an easy task, since most historians prefer a history of social processes, and most philosophers prefer a subject without history" ("About the Beginning of the Hermeneutics of the Self," p. 160). A genealogical view of subjectivity is Foucault's way out of such essentializing views of the human subject as a singular, transcendent entity.

In his later work, Foucault takes up the issue of the "**ethics of self.**" But ethics of self does not simply mean an individual's "morals." Rather, he is interested in identifying "techniques" or "technologies" of the self, that is, the regularized forms of behavior that constitute a particular human subject. Such technologies, which include sexual, political, legal, educational, and religious patterns of behavior, may be taken for granted—or even go completely unnoticed—by the subject who is constituted by them. Nonetheless, they function to *discipline* the body and mind within a larger order of power/knowledge. Techniques are subjectivizing practices that create and shape one's sense of self. These subjectivizing practices are not universal, but variable over time and place. By focusing on these technologies of the self, he aims to uncover how they are implicated in the construction of subjects.

For Foucault, technologies of the self are practices "which permit individuals to effect by their own means, or with the help of others, a certain number of operations on their own bodies and souls, thoughts, conduct, and way of being, so as to transform themselves in order to attain a certain state of happiness, purity, wisdom, perfection, or immortality" ("Technologies of the Self," p. 146). Significant here is the ethical idea that individuals can resist power and transform their own subjectivity by applying techniques of the self. While techniques of the self are about discipline, they are not simply about discipline as domination of the self; they also entail positive transformations of the self.

Foucault argues that morality has three references: (1) to a moral code, (2) to behaviors in relation to that code, and (3) to ways that a person conducts oneself. Foucault is primarily concerned with this last aspect. For him, self-conduct deals with how individuals view and create themselves as ethical subjects. This runs counter to notions of morality as measuring one's behavior against a transcendent moral code. In his three-volume study of sexuality, for instance, Foucault is interested in the question of how and why sexuality became an object of moral discourse as opposed to other areas—say, for example, food or exercise.

Many of Foucault's ideas have found a conceptual home in the academic study of religion. The questions and issues Foucault raises concerning such matters as discourse, genealogy, power, and knowledge are applicable to religious texts and practices. They also require us to move beyond traditional modernist descriptions of a religion's worldview or "essence" as expressed through theological/philosophical pronouncements and key rituals. Instead, following Foucault, we might ask if a religion's history constitutes a unified line back to an origin or whether the history of any religious tradition is always genealogical— incomplete, marked by rupture and power, "a field of tangled and confused parchments." Similarly, we might investigate ways in which religious traditions constitute communities of discourse that create religious subjects and implement technologies of the self in order to discipline bodies.

Although Foucault did not write extensively about religion, two volumes—one a study of the place of religion in Foucault's thought (Carrette, *Foucault and Religion*) and the other a companion collection of Foucault's writings, lectures, and interviews on religion (Foucault, *Religion and Culture*)—have attempted to redress the lack of scholarly attention given to Foucault's interests in religion, religious experience, and spirituality. Whether applying Foucault's theoretical perspectives to the study of religious texts and practices, or analyzing his explicit statements about religion, his work is an important point of departure for any consideration of the intersection of religion and culture.

Further Reading

By Foucault

Madness and Civilization: A History of Insanity in the Age of Reason. Translated by Richard Howard. New York: Vintage, 1973.

The Birth of the Clinic: An Archaeology of Medical Perception. Translated by A. M. Sheridan-Smith. New York: Pantheon, 1973.

The Order of Things: An Archaeology of the Human Sciences. Translated by Alan Sheridan. New York: Vintage, 1970.

The Archaeology of Knowledge. Translated by A. M. Sheridan-Smith. London: Tavistock, 1974

The History of Sexuality. Vol.I, An Introduction. Translated by Robert Hurley. New York: Vintage, 1978.

*"Nietzsche, Genealogy, History." In *Language, Counter-Memory, Practice: Selected Essays and Interviews*, edited by Donald F. Bourchard. Ithaca, NY: Cornell University Press, 1977.

*"The Subject and Power." Afterword to *Michel Foucault: Beyond Structuralism and Hermeneutics*, edited by Hubert L. Dreyfus and Paul Rabinow. Chicago: University of Chicago Press, 1983.

"Technologies of the Self." In *The Essential Foucault*, edited by Paul Rabinow and Nikolas Rose. New York: The New Press, 2003.

"About the Beginning of the Hermeneutics of the Self." In *Religion and Culture*, edited by Jeremy R. Carrette. London and New York: Routledge, 1999.

Religion and Culture. Edited by Jeremy R. Carrette. London and New York: Routledge, 1999.

About Foucault

*Carrette, Jeremy R. *Foucault and Religion: Spiritual Corporeality and Political Spirituality.* London and New York: Routledge, 2000.

Castelli, Elizabeth A. *Imitating Paul: A Discourse on Power.* Louisville, KY.: Westminster/John Knox Press, 1991.

Clark, Elizabeth A. "Foucault, the Fathers, and Sex." *Journal of the American Academy of Religion* 56 (1988): 619–41.

Danaher, Geoff, Tony Schirato, and Jen Webb. *Understanding Foucault.* London: Sage Publications, 2000.

Dreyfus, Hubert L., and Paul Rabinow. *Michel Foucault: Beyond Structuralism and Hermeneutics.* 2nd ed. Chicago: University of Chicago Press, 1983.

George, Mark K. "Assuming the Body of the Heir Apparent: David's Lament." In *Reading Bibles, Writing Bodies: Identity and the Book,* edited by David M. Gunn and Timothy K. Beal. London and New York: Routledge, 1996.

McNay, Lois. *Foucault and Feminism: Power, Gender, and the Self.* Boston: Northeastern University Press, 1992.

*Mills, Sara. *Michel Foucault.* London and New York: Routledge, 2003.

Moore, Stephen D. *Poststructuralism and the New Testament: Derrida and Foucault at the Foot of the Cross.* Minneapolis: Fortress Press, 1994.

HANS-GEORG GADAMER

Key Concepts

- hermeneutics
- effective history
- fusion of horizons
- prejudice
- religion of the world economy

Hans-Georg Gadamer (1900–2002) was born in Marburg, Germany. He studied philosophy and classical philology at University of Marburg, and earned his doctorate under the direction of Martin Heidegger in 1929. He held posts at the universities of Marburg, Leipzig, Frankfurt, and Heidelberg. Although he retired in 1968, he remained active in research and writing until his death in 2002. His complete collected works fill ten volumes.

Along with Heidegger and the philosopher of religion Paul Ricoeur, Gadamer is one of the most important twentieth-century scholars of **hermeneutics**, the science and art of interpretation, a field of study that has its ancient beginnings in Jewish and Christian scriptural studies. In Gadamer's work hermeneutics is transformed from the science of interpretation to the science of *understanding*. As such, it replaces metaphysics and epistemology as lords of the human sciences, addressing how humans find meaning and understand themselves and the world.

Gadamer's best-known and influential work is *Truth and Method*, published in German in 1960 and translated into English in 1975. There he develops a theory of understanding as linguistic and historical. Understanding takes form in language, and its form would be different if it were to develop in another linguistic field or according to other terms. Language is not simply a tool one uses to communicate, but the medium in which one lives and moves and has one's being. There is no understanding of oneself or of another without language. One is born and raised and formed as a subject within a language. Indeed, language is "the house of being." Likewise, there is no such thing as understanding that is not rooted in a particular historical context. Following Heidegger's concept of Being as *Dasein*, "there-being," Gadamer insists that human being is always already located, that is, "here." Human existence is always being-in-the-world, and there is no way for a human being to eradicate its historical-cultural situatedness from its understanding of anything. Gadamer describes this historical and linguistic situatedness of the human being as a person's *Wirkungsgeschichte*, or "**effective history**."

Yet there is another side to the hermeneutical event, another horizon. There is something—a work of art, a text, a cultural artifact, an idea—that is "other," that the human encounters and seeks to understand. Understanding is the process in which that "other" thing or idea or person is made meaningful, that is, understood. Gadamer describes this process of understanding as a **fusion of horizons**. On the one hand, there is the horizon of the one who wants to understand, located within that person's particular historical and linguistic context and shaped by its preexisting traditions, its effective history. On the other hand, there is the thing or person or text that someone is trying to understand. And that other horizon emerges from its own more or less unfamiliar historical and linguistic context. In the hermeneutical process, that is, the process of interpretation, the horizon of the interpreter fuses with that other horizon, creating a new dialogical meaning that is not identical to the monologue of the interpreter.

Gadamer's theory of understanding as historical and linguistic involves a critique of Enlightenment thought, with its ideal of the objective interpreter who remains detached from all cultural influences that threaten to **prejudice** one's understanding. For Gadamer, there is no such thing as unprejudiced understanding. Understanding always involves pre-understanding. We are always already historically situated, shaped by our culture and language, and that situatedness shapes our understandings of everything. We bring our own horizon, our own effective history, as a prejudice to any moment of understanding. For Gadamer, "the prejudices of the individual, far more than his judgments, constitute the historical reality of his being" (*Truth and Method,* p. 245).

Gadamer's rehabilitation of prejudice put his hermeneutical theory in direct conflict with the tradition of ideological critique, insofar as it suggested that there is no nonideological position from which to critique an ideology. This made Gadamer appear to some that he was returning to a precritical position and led to a now-famous series of debates with Jürgen Habermas, who contended that Gadamer's position does not adequately recognize the ways ideology can distort communication through the hidden expression of force (see Ricoeur, "Hermeneutics and the Critique of Ideology"). He also argued that Gadamer places too much weight on the power of our historical and linguistic context as that which constitutes us. Habermas, by contrast, called for more of an orientation toward the future, with an emancipatory interest in what ought to be rather than what was and is.

Although not a theorist of religion, Gadamer frequently applied his theory of hermeneutics to the study of religious myths and other scriptures (see, for instance, the essays collected in *Hermeneutics, Religion, and Ethics*). Late in life, at 92, he made a particularly significant contribution to a small symposium on religion organized by philosophers Jacques **DERRIDA** and Gianni Vattimo. A central topic for the conference was "Religion and the Religions," that is, the relation between universal ideas and theories of religion on the one hand and actual, historical religions as they are practiced on the other. Can we talk about "religion" in general? Is there such a thing as "religion?" In his contribution to the conference, "Dialogues in Capri," Gadamer makes two points that merit our attention here.

First, he raises the problem of "religion and the religions" vis-à-vis the emerging global economy. He suggests that scientific technology is taking on a life of its own as an "independent power over which we are no longer fully in control" and which "determines our destiny to an ever-increasing degree" (p. 202). As such, he suggests, it takes the form of a "**religion of the world economy**" (compare Derrida's point, in "Faith and Knowledge," that religion is the soul of the Western tele-technoscientific machine). Put this way, the obvious question emerges: what happens to particular, local religious communities and practices in the face of this technoscientific religious imperialism? "We must properly ask ourselves whether other religious and cultural worlds can provide any response to the universality of the scientific Enlightenment and its consequences which is different from the 'religion' of the global economy" (p. 204). Will this "religion," which now presses into every cultural corner of the globe, become the one universal religion? Can other more local, particular religious worldviews, practices, and institutions survive under its hegemonic pressures? Gadamer does not presume to predict. "We do not know whether the people who make up this larger part of humanity will be able successfully to defend their own religiously grounded social and cultural world under the thin and seemingly transparent industrial skin within which, to a greater or lesser extent, we all now live" (p. 203).

Second, regarding the search for a universal theory of religion (as opposed to a universal religion), Gadamer suggests that the one thing that all religions have in common is "the ubiquitous knowledge of one's own death and at the same time the impossibility of the actual experience of death" (p. 205). On the one hand, I know that I will die. On the other hand, I cannot actually experience that death, because my death is the end of me as a sentient, experiencing being. Religion, Gadamer proposes, is always in some sense about negotiating that tension, which is at the very core of what it is to be human.

Within the field of religious studies, Gadamer's work has been especially influential among theologians and historians of Christian thought. In particular, his hermeneutical theory has provided a conceptual framework for exploring how theological traditions (doctrines, rituals, scriptures) are reimagined and reconstituted in relation to new horizons of interpretation (see, for instance, Bryant, *Faith and the Play of Imagination*; Ricoeur, "Philosophical Hermeneutics and Theological Hermeneutics"; and Fiorenza, "Theory and Practice: Theological Education as a Reconstructive, Hermeneutical, and Practical Task"). Likewise, Gadamer has been useful in understanding preaching as a fusion of the horizons of Scripture on the one hand and the preacher and congregation on the other.

Beyond its apparent value for practical and historical theology within Christianity, Gadamer's theory of hermeneutics is valuable for the study of religion more generally in that it emphasizes the fact that a religious community is always in some sense an interpretive community, and that its interpretations are always unique fusions of horizons. Received traditions are always being transformed, and religion is always a dynamic of interpretation. In this way, Gadamer's hermeneutics emphasize religion as a dynamic, interpretive process rather than a fixed set of ideas and institutions.

Further Reading

By Gadamer

* *Truth and Method*. 2nd rev. ed. Translated by Garrett Barden and John Cumming. Revised translation by Joel Weinsheimer and Donald G. Marshall. New York: Crossroad, 1993.

* *Hermeneutics, Religion, and Ethics*. Edited and translated by Joel Weinsheimer. New Haven: Yale University Press, 1999.

Philosophical Hermeneutics. Edited by David E. Linge. Berkeley: University of California Press, 1976.

"Text and Interpretation." Translated by Dennis J. Schmidt. In *Hermeneutics and Modern Philosophy*, edited by Brice R. Wachterhauser. Albany: State University of New York Press, 1986.

"Dialogues in Capri." Translated by Jason Gaiger. In *Religion*, edited by Jacques Derrida and Gianni Vattimo. Stanford: Stanford University Press, 1998.

About Gadamer

Bryant, David J. *Faith and the Play of Imagination: On the Role of Imagination in Religion*. Macon: Mercer University Press, 1989.

Eberhard, Philippe. "The Mediality of Our Condition: A Christian Interpretation." *Journal of the American Academy of Religion* 67 (1999): 411–34.

Fiorenza, Francis Schussler. "Theory and Practice: Theological Education as a Reconstructive, Hermeneutical, and Practical Task." *Theological Education* 23 (1987): 113–41.

Miller, Vincent J. "History or Geography: Gadamer, Foucault, and Theologies of Tradition." *Theology and the New Histories*, edited by Gary Macy. Maryknoll: Orbis, 1999.

Ommen, Thomas B. "Bultmann and Gadamer: The Role of Faith in Theological Hermeneutics." *Thought* 59 (1984): 348–59.

*Ricoeur, Paul. "Hermeneutics and the Critique of Ideology." In *Hermeneutics and Modern Philosophy*, edited by Brice R. Wachterhauser. Albany: State University of New York Press, 1986.

———. "Philosophical Hermeneutics and Theological Hermeneutics." In *Philosophy of Religion and Theology*, translated by R. DeFord. Missoula: Scholars Press, 1975.

Schneiders, Sandra M. "The Foot Washing (John 13: 1–20): An Experiment in Hermeneutics." *Ex Auditu* 1 (1985): 135–46.

Schweiker, William. "Sacrifice, Interpretation, and the Sacred: The Import of Gadamer and Girard for Religious Studies." *Journal of the American Academy of Religion* 55 (1987): 791–810.

LUCE IRIGARAY

Key Concepts

- sexual difference
- specul(ariz)ation
- incarnation
- female mysticism (*mystérique*)

Luce Irigaray (1930–) was born in Belgium. She earned her master's degree from the University of Louvain in 1955 and then taught high school in Brussels until 1959. She moved to Paris where she earned a master's (1961) and then a diploma (1962) in psychology from the University of Paris. She attended Jacques **LACAN**'s seminars, became a member of his École Freudienne, and trained to become an analyst. In 1968 she also received her doctorate in linguistics, which led to a teaching position at the University of Vincennes (1970–74). She was expelled from Jacques Lacan's École and lost her faculty post at Vincennes after publishing *Speculum of the Other Woman* (1974), her second doctoral thesis. She is currently director of research at the Centre National de la Recherche Scientifique in Paris.

Unlike some other French feminists with which she is frequently identified (especially **KRISTEVA**), Irigaray has consistently held that there is in fact such a thing as **sexual difference** and that female sexual identity is autonomous and unique, grounded in women's specific embodied experiences (a position sometimes called "difference feminism").

In *Speculum of the Other Woman* and other early works, such as *This Sex Which Is Not One* (collected essays first published in 1977), she argues that Western intellectual tradition has essentially elided the feminine, positing it not on its own terms, but in relation to, or rather over against, the masculine as the normative human identity. "Woman" in Western discourse has largely been defined as man's other. Mimicking the discourses of **FREUD**, Plato, and other intellectuals writing "about women"—what are they? where do they come from? what are they for?—she demonstrates how "woman" functions primarily as an idea that clarifies "man," that is, man's other/opposite. She describes this in terms of a process of **specul(ariz)ation**, that is, a process of male speculation about woman as man's other that associates her with a series of other terms and concepts within a larger set of oppositions that organize the Western patriarchal symbolic order (see **LACAN** in this volume). Within this set of structural oppositions or "interpretive modalities" that shape our understanding of the world, woman and the feminine are associated in each pairing with the negative terms: light–dark, in–out, heavens–earth, and especially phallus–lack, original–derivative, positive–negative, and active–passive. She writes: "All these are interpretive modalities of the female function rigorously postulated by the pursuit of a certain game for which she will always find herself signed up without having begun to play. . . . A reserve supply of negativity sustaining the articulation of their moves, or refusals to move, in a partly fictional progress toward the mastery of power" (*Speculum*, p. 22). Elsewhere she states: "The 'feminine' is always described in terms of deficiency or atrophy, as the other side of the sex that alone holds monopoly on value: the male sex" (*This Sex Which Is Not One*, p. 69).

Working against this symbolic reduction of woman to the "other side" of man, Irigaray asserts the non-oppositional difference of a real embodied other woman. Here, woman is not reducible to man's other-opposite; her otherness refuses to be reduced to an object of exchange within the male sexual economy. This is an otherness with agency that is unpredictable and irreducible to the male economy. As such, her voice and action and way of seeing (not simply talked about, acted upon, and seen) have subversive power within that economy to bring about a "disaggregation" of the privileged male/masculine subject of Western discourse and society (*Speculum*, 135). Thus woman's subjectivity, as other, can bring about a collapse of the binary logic of the male symbolic order, thereby opening up new possibilities of social relations.

From her earliest work, Irigaray has been interested in issues of sexual difference in religious discourse, especially within Christianity. On the one hand, she recognizes that these discourses have served the patriarchal order of the West very well, providing divine legitimation for conceiving of woman as man's other and negative image. In "Women, the Sacred, and Money," she focuses in particular on the centrality of sacrifice within Western culture, arguing that the most foundational sacrificial act within this culture is the sacrifice of women and women's work to the masculine symbolic and social economy. Against this sacrificial order, of which men are the high priests, Irigaray calls for a new religion freed from the structures of debt and sacrifice. She makes a similar point in *Marine Lover of Friedrich Nietzsche*, in which she shows how **NIETZSCHE** appropriates the feminine and maternal in ways that enable him to forget actual women and mothers. This book concludes with a long poetic reflection on Jesus and Dionysus. Despite Nietzsche's own powerful critique of Christianity, Irigaray argues that he inadvertently reinscribes Christianity's denial and forgetting of real women's bodies: whereas the incarnation is about the "word made flesh," Western Christian tradition is the story of the reversal of that incarnation, that is, the flesh made word.

Irigaray has also sometimes looked to religion for ways of breaking free from the dominant structures of patriarchy in the West. She recognizes the power of religion, particularly theology, to reconceive the world and human identities and relationships within it. In "Divine Women," she argues that the divine needs to be reimagined in ways that do not elide the feminine. There she calls for women to envision a divine feminine rooted in their own embodied experiences. Indeed, she believes that such a reimagining of God is crucial to the development and affirmation of a genuine feminine subjectivity in contemporary society.

Within traditional Christian thought, Irigaray has been especially interested in theology of the **incarnation**, the physical, fleshly embodiment of the divine in the world. In taking the body seriously as the site of God's coming into the world, born of a woman, incarnational theology has the potential to affirm the uniquely embodied experiences of women. Her essay "La Mystérique" in the center of *Speculum*, for example, reflects on **female mysticism** as expressed in the religious devotional practices of women mystics—especially Teresa of Avila—presenting mysticism as subversive of the more ideological, heady speculations of dogmatics and systematic theology, which readily serve the patriarchal symbolic order. She sees mysticism as the domain of the feminine within religion insofar as it provides a subject position from which women may speak without denying their own embodied experience. Teresa of Avila's religious practice is, paradoxically, a kind of self-transcendence rooted in bodily experience. Thus her practice breaks down the conceptual opposition of transcendence-immanence so central to much of Western thought. In Teresa's meditations on the suffering and death of Christ, moreover, Irigaray sees a conception of Christ as "that most female of men" (*Speculum*, p. 199) who, in the incarnation, is an image of the divine that has descended from heaven to earth after having abandoned all attributes of divine omnipotence and omniscience.

Given her strong interest in reimagining the divine vis-à-vis traditional Christian theological tradition, it is not surprising that, among religionists, her work has been most fruitfully engaged by feminist theologians (e.g., Armour, Gardner, Anderson, Ward, and Jantzen). Beyond her value in that field, her critique of the "classic" discourses of Western philosophy and psychoanalysis offers religionists a model for much-needed critical analyses of classic texts within the discourse of academic religious studies (Tylor, Durkheim, Eliade, etc.). There is a great need for religious studies that can identify and interrogate the "interpretive modalities" developed within those texts that remain so influential on contemporary discourse about religion and the religious.

Further Reading
By Irigaray

Speculum of the Other Woman. Translated by Gillian C. Gill. Ithaca: Cornell University Press, 1985.

This Sex Which Is Not One. Translated by Catherine Porter. Ithaca: Cornell University Press, 1985.

"Women, the Sacred, and Money." In *Sexes and Genealogies*, translated by Gillian C. Gill. Ithaca: Cornell University Press, 1993.

"Divine Women." In *Sexes and Genealogies*, translated by Gillian C. Gill. Ithaca: Cornell University Press, 1993.

Marine Lover of Friedrich Nietzsche. Translated by Gillian C. Gill. New York: Columbia University Press, 1991.

About Irigaray

Ainley, Alison. "Luce Irigaray: Divine Spirit and Feminine Space." In *Post-secular Philosophy: Between Philosophy and Theology*, edited by Phillip Blond. London and New York: Routledge, 1998.

Armour, Ellen T. *Deconstruction, Feminist Theology, and the Problem of Difference: Subverting the Race/Gender Divide*. Chicago: University of Chicago Press, 1999.

Berry, Philippa. "Woman and Space According to Kristeva and Irigaray." In *Shadow of Spirit: Postmodernism and Religion*, edited by Philippa Berry and Andrew Wernick. London and New York: Routledge, 1992.

Bible and Culture Collective. "Psychoanalysis and Feminism: Kristeva and Irigaray." In *The Postmodern Bible*. New Haven: Yale University Press, 1997.

Bodde, Ree. "A God of Her Own." *Feminist Theology* 19 (1998): 48–62.

Deutscher, Penelope. "The Only Diabolical Thing about Women . . . Luce Irigaray on Divinity." *Hypatia* 9 (1994): 88–112.

Gardner, Lucy. "Touching upon the Soul: The Interiority of Transcendence after Luce Irigaray." In *Challenging Women's Orthodoxies in the Context of Faith*, edited by Susan Frank Parsons. Burlington: Ashgate, 2000.

Grosz, Elizabeth. "Irigaray and the Divine." In *Transfigurations: Theology and the French Feminists*, edited by C. W. Maggie Kim, Susan St. Ville, and Susan M. Simonaitis. Minneapolis: Fortress Press, 1993.

*Hollywood, Amy. "Deconstructing Belief: Irigaray and the Philosophy of Religion." *Journal of Religion* 78 (1998): 230–45.

Jaarsma, Ada S. "Irigaray's To Be Two: The Problem of Evil and the Plasticity of Incarnation." *Hypatia* 18 (2003): 44–62.

Jantzen, Grace M. "'Barely by a Breath . . .': Irigaray on Rethinking Religion." In *The Religious*, edited by John D. Caputo. Oxford: Blackwell, 2002.

*Joy, Morny, Kathleen O'Grady, and Judith L. Poxon, eds. *French Feminists on Religion: A Reader*. London and New York: Routledge, 2002.

Kaminski, Phyllis H. "Mysticism Embodied Differently: Luce Irigaray and the Subject of Incarnate Love." *Religious Studies and Theology* 17 (1998): 59–79.

Priest, Ann-Marie. "Woman as God, God as Woman: Mysticism, Negative Theology, and Luce Irigaray." *Journal of Religion* 83 (2003): 1–23.

Ward, Graham. "Divinity and Sexuality: Luce Irigaray and Christology." *Modern Theology* 12 (1996): 221–37.

JULIA KRISTEVA

Key Concepts

- semiotic/*chora*
- signifying process
- intertextuality
- subject in process
- abjection

Julia Kristeva (1940–) is a psychoanalyst and feminist theorist of language and literature. Born in Bulgaria, she moved to Paris in 1966 on a doctoral research fellowship. There, she quickly became involved in the leftist intellectual movement that congregated around the literary journal *Tel Quel*. Her most influential teacher during that time was Roland **BARTHES**. Her doctoral thesis, *Revolution in Poetic Language*, was published in 1974 and led to her appointment to a chair in linguistics at the University of Paris VII, where she has remained throughout her academic career. Since 1979 she has also maintained a practice as a psychoanalyst.

Kristeva works at the intersection of linguistics, psychoanalysis, and feminist theory. She has written on numerous topics, from horror to love to depression. Overall, her interests lie less in the formal structures of language and meaning than in what escapes and disrupts—the unrepresentable, inexpressible other within language, within the self, and within society. There, she sees the possibility for revolutionary social transformation.

In *Revolution in Poetic Language*, Kristeva refers to the potentially revolutionary otherness within language as the **semiotic**, or ***chora***, which is in tension with the symbolic, or *thetic*. This semiotic is decipherable within language (especially in poetic language), yet it is in tension with the dominant symbolic order (see **LACAN**) that governs language. In psychoanalytic terms, the semiotic or *chora* is associated with the prelinguistic phase and the mother's body. Indeed, Kristeva associates this choratic element in poetic language with the mother, the child, prelinguistic babbling, and so on (see especially her early memoir of motherhood,

"Stabat Mater"). It exists within language, especially poetic language, as a potentially subversive force. The semiotic can never be entirely constrained by the symbolic; it perpetually infiltrates the symbolic construction of meaning and so reintroduces fluidity and heterogeneity within the speaking/writing subject. It reopens the process of creation. Kristeva describes it as the "very precondition" of symbolic order (*Revolution in Poetic Language*, p. 50). Insofar as the symbolic order of language is identified with consciousness, we can think of the semiotic or *chora* as language's unconscious. The infiltration of the semiotic within language is the return of the linguistically repressed. Notice that Kristeva's concept of the semiotic differs from its standard meaning of semiotics as the science of signs.

In *Revolution in Poetic Language* and other works, Kristeva focuses on the **signifying process** more than its product. She reads a text in order to discover not only the processes by which it comes to gain meaning (*signify*), but also what within the text resists and undermines that process (see also Kristeva's "Semiotics" and "The System and the Speaking Subject"). In this respect, we can think of her method of literary analysis as a kind of psychoanalysis of texts, not taking their final, fixed state for granted but looking into them in order to explore how they came into being, how they came to say what they say, as well as what was repressed in the process and what within them keeps them fundamentally unstable. In this way, her analysis seeks those places in language that open to the possibility of social transformation, "the production of a different kind of subject, one capable of bringing about new social relations, and thus joining in the process of capitalism's subversion" (*Revolution in Poetic Language*, p. 105).

Kristeva's theory of **intertextuality** has had a tremendous influence on literary studies, less so on philosophy and religion. This theory was developed in relation to Mikhail **BAKHTIN**'s concept of dialogism. The idea of intertextuality first appears in her 1969 essay, "Word, Dialogue and the Novel," as part of a larger critique of modern conceptions of texts as discrete, self-enclosed containers of meaning. Contrary to this conception, intertextuality draws attention to the fact that every text is "constructed as a mosaic of quotations" ("Word, Dialogue, and Novel," p. 66). It is a "field of transpositions of various signifying systems (an inter-textuality)" (*Revolution in Poetic Language,* p. 60), an "*intersection of textual surfaces* rather than a point (a fixed meaning)" ("Word, Dialogue, and Novel," p. 65).

Within religious studies, intertextuality offers a way of conceiving of texts and traditions that challenges their categorization into the canonical and noncanonical. To recognize the Christian Bible as an intertextuality, for example, is to recognize that it cannot be separated from the various textual fields— ancient as well as contemporary—that are its contexts. In this sense, there is no such thing as a closed canon.

Another key concept in Kristeva's work that has obvious implications for religious studies is **abjection** (see especially *Powers of Horror*, first published in French in 1980). The abject is that which does not fit within the social and symbolic order of things, and which therefore must be excluded from that order, declared unclean or impure and pushed outside the boundaries. Always threatening to break back into that order and contaminate it, the abject must be kept at bay. Abjection, then, is the process by which a society identifies the abject and excludes it from its order through various prohibitions and taboos. As such, abjection serves to define the boundaries of the social-symbolic order.

In *Powers of Horror*, and later in her essay on "Reading the Bible" (first published in French in 1993), Kristeva finds the laws and prohibitions of the Book of Leviticus to be particularly revealing as a process of abjection. Leviticus, she argues, is a "logicizing of what departs from the symbolic" (*Powers of Horror*, p. 91). It begins with the foundational opposition of humanity and God and develops from there a "complete system of logical oppositions" (*Powers of Horror*, pp. 98–99). Within this system, "the pure will be that which conforms to an established taxonomy" and the impure, or abject, will be "that which unsettles it, establishes intermixture and disorder" (*Powers of Horror*, p. 99).

According to Kristeva's analysis, the symbolic order in Leviticus is shown to be a patriarchal and xenophobic system with an adult male as its privileged subject. As such, its divinely sanctioned commands and prohibitions serve to subordinate all "maternal power" to its rule (*Powers of Horror*, p. 91). Thus the biblical "God" is conceived as the author and guarantor of this system, the fundamental purpose of which is to prohibit identification with the mother. Indeed, Kristeva sees the taboo of the mother is the "originating mytheme" of the order constructed in Leviticus (*Powers of Horror*, p. 106) and finds traces of this taboo in the prohibition against boiling a kid in its mother's milk as well as in the command for circumcision, by which the son becomes dissociated from the mother and identified with the father (who in turn is identified with the Father-God, and therefore with patriarchal order).

In many respects, Kristeva's analysis of Levitical dietary laws is akin to anthropologist Mary Douglas's well-known analysis in *Purity and Danger*. But whereas Douglas focuses exclusively on how these prohibitions work to structure ancient Israelite culture according to a particular symbolic order, Kristeva insists that we need to move beyond that focus in order to ask how this order constructs a particular kind of human subjectivity. Reading the Bible as a "strategy of identity" ("Reading the Bible," p. 94), she wants to examine not only the system presented in Leviticus but also the text's "speaking subject," that is, its narrator. When the text is approached in this way, Kristeva argues, we may gain insight into the *process* of subject formation, which is never final and always open to breakdown through the return of the repressed (see also

Beal, "Opening," in which the biblical God is also understood to be a subject at risk in the same way).

Throughout her career, Kristeva has been interested in women's religious experience and the sacred. In a series of published conversations with anthropologist and feminist theorist Catherine Clément, she focuses on whether one can conceive of the sacred in strictly feminine terms (*The Feminine and the Sacred*, based on conversations between the two in 1996). Without developing a specific theory of the sacred, this conversation between Kristeva and Clément raises provocative questions about whether women's religious experience is particularly open to the interrelationship of faith and sexuality, the mystical, and the sensual.

Further Reading

By Kristeva

The Kristeva Reader. Edited by Toril Moi. New York: Columbia University Press, 1986.

"Stabat Mater." In *The Kristeva Reader,* Edited by Toril Moi. New York: Columbia University Press, 1986.

Revolution in Poetic Language. Abridged and translated by Margaret Waller. New York: Columbia University Press, 1984.

Powers of Horror: An Essay on Abjection. Translated by L.S. Roudiez. New York: Columbia University Press, 1982.

Tales of Love. Translated by L.S. Roudiez. New York: Columbia University Press, 1987.

"The System and the Speaking Subject." In *The Kristeva Reader*, edited by Toril Moi. New York: Columbia University Press, 1986.

"Semiotics: A Critical Science and/or a Critique of Science." In *The Kristeva Reader*, edited by Toril Moi. New York: Columbia University Press, 1986.

"Word, Dialogue and the Novel." In *Desire in Language: A Semiotic Approach to Literature and Art*, edited by Leon Roudiez. New York: Columbia University Press, 1980.

"Reading the Bible." In *New Maladies of the Soul*, translated by R. Guberman. New York: Columbia University Press, 1995.

(with Catherine Clément) *The Feminine and the Sacred.* Translated by Jane Marie Todd. New York: Columbia University Press, 2001.

About Kristeva

Astell, Ann W. "Telling Tales of Love: Julia Kristeva and Bernard of Clairvaux." *Christianity and Literature* 50 (2000): 125–48.

Beal, Timothy K. "Opening: Cracking the Binding." *Reading Bibles, Writing Bodies: Identity and the Book*, edited by David M. Gunn and Timothy K. Beal. London and New York: Routledge, 1997.

Berry, Philippa. "Kristeva's Feminist Refiguring of the Gift." In *Post-Secular Philosophy*, edited by Phillip Blond. London and New York: Routledge, 1998.

Chopp, Rebecca S. "From Patriarchy into Freedom: A Conversation between American Feminist Theology and French Feminism." In *Transfigurations*, edited by Susan St. Ville, Susan M. Simonaitis, and C. W. Maggie Kim. Minneapolis: Fortress Press, 1993.

Jasper, Alison. "Communicating: The Word of God." *Journal for the Study of the New Testament* 20 (1997): 29–45.

*Joy, Morny, Kathleen O'Grady, and Judith L. Poxon, eds. *French Feminists on Religion: A Reader.* London and New York: Routledge, 2002.

Kearns, Cleo McNelly. "Kristeva and Feminist Theology." In *Transfigurations*, edited by Susan St. Ville, Susan M. Simonaitis, and C. W. Maggie Kim. Minneapolis: Fortress Press, 1993.

O'Grady, Kathleen. "The Pun or the Eucharist? Eco and Kristeva on the Consummate Model for the Metaphoric Process," *Literature and Theology* 11 (1997): 93–115.

JACQUES LACAN

Key Concepts

- symbolic order
- unconscious
- Real
- Imaginary
- mirror stage
- desire
- phallus/castration

Jacques Lacan (1901–1981) was born in Paris to a Roman Catholic family. He earned a medical degree at the Sorbonne and then trained as a psychoanalyst. His relationship with mainstream psychoanalysis in Europe was tense, and he resigned from the Société psychanalytique de Paris in 1953—the same year he gave his famous lecture "The Function and Field of Speech and Language" at the International Psychoanalytic Association in Rome (also referred to as "The Rome Discourse"). It was also that same year that he inaugurated his weekly seminar, which continued almost until his death in 1981. Lacan's seminar was the primary venue for sharing his work. Most of his published essays were originally given as papers in this seminar, which was attended by many intellectuals, including Julia **KRISTEVA** and Luce **IRIGARAY**. In 1963 he founded the École Freudienne de Paris.

Focused on the formation of the subject and the role of the unconscious, Lacan's work constitutes a radical reinterpretation of **FREUD** and psychoanalysis in light of structuralism (especially the structural linguistics of **SAUSSURE** and the structural anthropology of Levi-Strauss). Dissenting from the common conception, widespread among his contemporaries (and championed especially by Heinz Hartmann), of the ego, or conscious self, as autonomous, sovereign, and biologically determined, Lacan theorized that it was formed within a preexisting symbolic order, interpolated within a system of meaning that it had no part in creating. Far from autonomous and sovereign, it becomes a subject, an ego, an "I," when it is *subjected* to a preexisting **symbolic order**. The **unconscious**, moreover, is not a biologically determined realm of libidinal drives; rather, it is formed in tandem with the formation of ego. It is a side effect of the ego's subjection within the symbolic order. It is created as the excess, the surplus of self that does not fit within the subject as it is formed by the symbolic order. Thus the unconscious reveals the fact that we as subjects are always more and other than our social selves allow. The unconscious reveals our "toomuchness," the fact that we are split selves. Far from being an autonomous, sovereign agent in the world, then, the ego is an illusion, a symbolically constructed selfhood whose excesses, splits, and gaps are revealed by the eruptions of the unconscious into conscious life.

Lacan develops this understanding of ego formation and the unconscious vis-à-vis the structural linguistics of Saussure. For Lacan, the birth of subjectivity is one's entry into language, understood as a synchronic system of signs and social codes that generate meaning, that is, a symbolic order. It is this symbolic order that locates you, forms you, "subjects" you, thereby enabling you to become an acting subject. Before Lacan, most psychoanalysts believed that the development of the ego as the seat of consciousness was a biological development. Lacan argued that it was a linguistic–symbolic development. Birth into language is birth into subjectivity. As he famously pronounced in "The Function and Field of Language," "Man speaks, then, but it is because the symbol has made him man" (p. 65). And later in the same essay he states:

> Symbols in fact envelop the life of man in a network so total that they join together, before he comes into the world, those who are going to engender him "by flesh and blood"; so total that they bring to his birth, along with the gifts of the stars, if not with the gifts of the fairies, the shape of his destiny; so total that they give the words that will make him faithful or renegade, the law of the acts that will follow him right to the very place where he *is* not yet and even beyond his death; and so total that through them his end finds its meaning in the last judgment, where the Word absolves his being or condemns it. . . . (p. 68)

The subject emerges from its nonindividuated, prelinguistic state of being not into unmediated reality but into a culturally constructed world of symbols, a symbolic order. The subject is constituted by the symbolic order, which has, as **SLAVOJ ŽIŽEK** puts it, colonized the live body like a parasite (*The Fragile Absolute*, p. 91). Although conscious human existence is thus culturally constructed through language, the subject does not recognize it as such, but experiences (or rather imagines) it to be reality itself.

Lacan uses the term **Real** in reference to that which is really "there," "in its place" apart from the symbolic order and outside its ordering of things. It is the present, as opposed to that which is re-presented through language in the symbolic order. The human subject, constituted by the symbolic order, is radically alienated from the Real. As such, it is unattainable.

A crucial stage in this development, according to Lacan, is the subject's entry into the **Imaginary**, which is closely related to the mirror stage (for a clear discussion of both, see "The Mirror Stage as Formative of the Function of the I as Revealed in Psychoanalytic Experience," first presented in 1949). The Imaginary precedes the child's entry into the symbolic order and continues to operate along with it throughout one's life. The Imaginary is the order according to which the child becomes aware of itself as an "I," a subject, among other subjects. It is the general matrix of self and other.

Lacan identifies the **mirror stage** as an important means by which the child is inaugurated into the Imaginary. The mirror stage occurs between the ages of six and eighteen months, when the child first recognizes itself in a mirror as a coherent whole self, like other selves. In this moment, before the child can speak or even walk, the child recognizes itself as an "I." Yet this recognition is in fact a misrecognition, for it is a recognition of itself *as other*, an objectification of itself in an image whose point of view and position are outside itself. In this respect, the mirror stage, which inaugurates the Imaginary, may be seen as "one of those crises of alienation around which the Lacanian subject is organized, since to know oneself through an external image is to be defined through self-alienation" (Siverman, p. 158).

According to Lacan's narrative of child development, the child's entry into language as a subject coincides with its separation from the mother. The mother, therefore, is the child's first experience of lack—absence—which creates the condition of **desire**. The father intervenes in the mother–child relationship at a moment coinciding with the child's entry into the symbolic order and loss of union with the mother. As the child becomes a subject within the symbolic order, the father is identified with that order which constitutes and governs subjectivity. For this reason, Lacan sometimes called the symbolic order *le Nom-du-Père* ("the Name of the Father"), which in French is pronounced the same as *le Non-du-Père* ("the No of the Father"), thus signifying God-like authority and prohibition. Thus the child is *subjected* in both senses of the word: subjected to the law of the symbolic order (identified with patriarchal law/no of the father) and constituted as an acting subject in the world.

This is where the **phallus** comes in, so to speak. One of the first childhood experiences of sexual difference, according to Lacan as well as Freud, is the recognition that the mother does not have a penis. But for Lacan, what is most important is the *symbolic* significance of the penis, a significance he emphasizes by consistently using the term "phallus." What matters in the symbolic order is not the body part, but what it signifies. First, it signifies sexual difference. Second, insofar as the father (identified with the symbolic order) has a penis and the mother (identified with the prelinguistic state of bliss before entry into the symbolic order) does not, the phallus signifies lack/absence within the symbolic order. For Lacan, the phallus comes to signify *both* women's and men's lack, dependence, and subjective vulnerability within the symbolic order. The father may be identified by the child with the symbolic, but he too was once a child, subjected to the same law and always inadequate and incomplete in relation to it, never in full possession of it. No one possesses the phallus. All are "**castrated**." As feminist biblical scholar Deborah Krause puts it, "castration is an equal opportunity employer."

Some scholars of religion and gender find Lacan useful because he insists that there is nothing essential about the androcentric symbolic order with its foundational patriarchal structures of sexual difference. For Lacan, there is nothing essential or "natural" about sexual difference itself. Woman, man, femininity, and masculinity are symbolic constructions formed arbitrarily by a repressive system of meaning that masquerades as the Real.

As mentioned earlier, the unconscious is formed at the same time as the subject/ego. It is an effect of the repression that takes place during subjection. Ego formation requires repression of whatever does not fit within the symbolic order—whatever exceeds it. The unconscious is "the censored chapter" in the history of psychic life ("The Function and Field of Speech and Language in Psychoanalysis," p. 50). It is an otherness within—in Freudian terms, the *unheimlich*, the "unhomely" that remains, closeted, in the home of selfhood— manifesting itself in and through language, often as interruption—mispeakings, slips, and forgetting names. And when it does so, it pokes holes in the subject and its world, potentially revealing its illusory nature. In other words, the in-breaking of the unconscious within conscious existence reveals the fact that the subject is a tentative construction, by no means entirely stable or permanent and not entirely whole. In Lacan's words, "the unconscious is that part of the concrete discourse . . . that is not at the disposal of the subject in re-establishing the continuity of his conscious discourse" ("The Function and Field of Speech and Language in Psychoanalysis," p. 49). It is an in-breaking that may open one's consciousness to the possibility that the Real is elsewhere, lost beyond one's grasp.

How might religion be understood vis-à-vis Lacan? On the one hand, as suggested by the biblical connotation of Lacan's "Law of the Father," religion might be conceived as the patriarchal regulator and guarantor of the symbolic order, that which governs primordial, prelinguistc existence and keeps the Real at bay. Durkheim's characterization of religion as a "necessary illusion" seems to push in this direction. On the other hand, it might be suggested that what is called religious experience, that is, the experience of the wholly other, or the sacred, or the mysterium, is in fact an in-breaking of the Real by way of the agency of the unconscious. To approach the phenomenon of religious experience in this way, from a Lacanian psychoanalytic perspective, would suggest that it is an encounter with otherness that is within as much as without. Such an *unheimlich* other within would thus be understood not as an encounter with transcendence but as an effect of repression. Yet, as such, it is also a symptom of a Real that is fundamentally beyond our rational existence.

Further Reading

By Lacan

*"The Function and Field of Speech and Language in Psychoanalysis." In *Ecrits: A Selection*, translated by Alan Sheridan. London: Tavistock, 1977.

*"The Mirror Stage as Formative of the Function of the I as Revealed in Psychoanalytic Experience." In *Ecrits: A Selection*, translated by Alan Sheridan. London: Tavistock, 1977.

"The Signification of the Phallus." In *Ecrits: A Selection*, translated by Alan Sheridan. London: Tavistock, 1977.

"The Agency of the Letter in the Unconscious or Reason since Freud." In *Ecrits: A Selection*, translated by Alan Sheridan. London: Tavistock, 1977.

Four Fundamental Concepts of Psychoanalysis. Translated by Alan Sheridan. New York: Norton, 1978.

About Lacan

Bible and Culture Collective. *The Postmodern Bible*. New Haven: Yale University Press, 1997.

DiCenso, James J. *The Other Freud: Religion, Culture, and Psychoanalysis*. London and New York: Routledge, 1999.

*Evans, Dylan. *Introductory Dictionary of Lacanian Psychoanalysis*. New York and London: Routledge,1996.

Halpern, Richard. "Creation: Lacan in Kansas." *Journal for Cultural and Religious Theory* 2 (2000): <www.jcrt.org/archives/02.1/halpern.shtml>.

Raschke, Carl A. "God and Lacanian Psychoanalysis: Toward a Reconsideration of the Discipline of Religious Studies." In *Religion, Society, and Psychoanalysis: Readings in Contemporary Theory*, edited by Donald Capps and Janet Liebman Jacobs. Boulder, Colo.: Westview Press, 1997.

Roustang, François. *Dire Mastery: Discipleship from Freud to Lacan*. Translated by Ned Lukacher. Baltimore: Johns Hopkins University Press, 1999.

Silverman, Kaja. *The Subject of Semiotics*. Oxford: Oxford University Press, 1983.

Winquist, Charles. "Lacan and Theology." In *Post-Secular Philosophy: Between Philosophy and Theology*, edited by Phillip Blond. London and New York: Routledge, 1998.

Wyschogrod, Edith, David Crownfield, and Cark A. Raschke, Eds. *Lacan and Theological Discourse* Albany: State University of New York Press, 1989.

Zizek, Slavoj. *The Fragile Absolute Or, Why Is the Christian Legacy Worth Fighting for?* London: Verso, 2000.

HENRI LEFEBVRE

Key Concepts

- everyday life
- perceived space
- conceived space
- lived space

Henri Lefebvre (1901–91) was a French Marxist social theorist, philosopher, and historian. Born and raised in the Landes region of southwestern France, he studied philosophy in Paris, where he became involved with a group of, young intellectuals promoting Marxist ideas. He joined the French Communist Party (Parti Communiste Français, or PCF) in 1928. He was influenced by Marx's early writings, some of which he translated into French. He fought in the French resistance during World War II. Afterward, he became a broadcaster and devoted his time to writing about Marxism, though he regularly skirmished with the PCF over his "humanist" Marxist views that were based, in part, on the Hegel-influenced early writings of Marx. Lefebvre was expelled from the French Communist Party in 1958 because of his anti-Stalinist views (though he became involved again in the late 1970s).

Later, in the 1950s, Lefebvre was appointed to a research position in sociology. It was during this time that he applied Marxist ideas to the sociology of everyday life. He went on to hold sociology chairs, first at Strasbourg and then at Nanterre, from which he played an active role in the 1968 Paris protests. It was during this period that he explored new intellectual currents, embracing ideas taken from sociology, literary criticism, and philosophy.

Lefebvre was antagonistic toward the linguistic and anthropological structuralisms popular among French intellectuals in the 1960s and wrote articles criticizing the work of Claude Lévi-Strauss and Michel **FOUCAULT**. He also critiqued the antihumanist Marxist views of Louis **ALTHUSSER**, accusing him of turning structuralism into an ideology.

Lefebvre was the author of more than sixty books, although much of this work has yet to be translated into English. His scholarship has influenced such diverse disciplines as philosophy, sociology, literature, geography, and political science and has been championed by postmodern spatial theorists, among others. Lefebvre's major intellectual contributions concern the study of "everyday life" and the configuration of social space in capitalist urban settings.

In his own lifetime, Lefebvre was witness to the rise of industrialism in France and, along with it, the increasing urbanization and suburbanization of French life. These experiences informed his application of Marxist critical theory to problems of **everyday life**. Lefebvre draws attention to the social forms of alienation that appear in the quotidian affairs of human beings as a result of capitalist modernization. For Lefebvre, this alienation is the product of a three-stage process. In the first stage, everyday human activities are spontaneously ordered and largely independent of the state. This spontaneity is then co-opted in the second stage by capitalist forms of rational structure. Finally, in the third stage, these co-opted forms of everyday activity become systems of oppression. Economically, Lefebvre argues, divisions of labor become means for worker exploitation. Similarly, benign political structures become oppressive state ideologies.

In the three volumes of *The Critique of Everyday Life* (the first volume was published in French in 1958), Lefebvre delineates the alienating effects of capitalism and urbanization on everyday life. He argues that within capitalist society, human beings lose control of their own self-actualization (as subjects) and increasingly describe themselves as objects within the economic system (as, for instance, "assets" and "consumers"). They objectify and commodify themselves in economic terms and thus become alienated from their own lives.

In *The Production of Space* (1974), Lefebvre turned his critical attention to an analysis of social space. He is concerned not only with how social space is produced within a social context, but also with how particular forms of space actually produce the forms of life that take place within them. Space is not simply an external location that human occupants act upon and shape, as we so often assume. Rather, space is a subject that acts upon and shapes us and our social lives.

Lefebvre reads space primarily from a Marxist perspective. He is interested in transcending a bipartite view of space as physical form—**perceived space**—and mental construct—**conceived space**. To this end, Lefebvre proposes a three-tiered analysis of space, one which adds a dimension that he refers to as **lived space**. Lefebvre organizes his trivalent spatial analysis in the following way:

The fields we are concerned with are, first, the *physical*—nature, the Cosmos; secondly, the *mental*, including logical and formal abstractions; and, thirdly, the *social*. In other words, we are concerned with logico-epistemological space, the space of social practice, the space occupied by sensory phenomena, including products of the imagination such as projects and projections, symbols and utopias. (*The Production of Space*, pp. 11–12).

This tripartite view of space is understood *not* as three compartmentalized spaces—space separable into three—but is conceived as a synthesis of all three. All territory comprises of all three aspects of space at once. Lefebvre charts his view of space in terms of the interconnections between the three categories of space. The following table summarizes the terms he uses to name these three kinds of space along with the meaning assigned to these terms.

Lefebvre's terms		Meaning
physical space	• perceived space • spatial practice	• physical, material space
mental space	• conceived space • representations of space	• concepts/ideas about space
social space	• lived space • spaces of representation	• space as experienced (physically, emotionally, intellectually, ideologically, etc.)

Edward Soja (*Thirdspace*) has taken up Lefebvre's spatial trialectics, developing his three categories in terms of Firstspace, Secondspace, and Thirdspace. For Soja, Thirdspace (Lefebvre's social space) is a combination of Firstspace (physical space) and Secondspace (mental space). Thirdspace, then, cannot be separated from the others and must be examined together with them. Firstspace (physical space) is also always Secondspace (mental space) and Thirdspace (social space). When one looks out over a natural (physical) landscape, one does so through a conceptual spatial lens, and one experiences that landscape as lived space. Likewise, one's experience of space (as lived space) is an experience of a conceptualized physical space. In approaching lived space in this way, Soja seeks to move beyond the binary logic of either/or into a trialectical logic of both/and.

A simple example may help clarify Soja's theoretical spatial distinctions vis-à-vis Lefebvre. Consider the space you are occupying as you read this text. The physical space—dimensions of a room, furniture, window placement, temperature, etc.—is perceived space, the space presented to you through your five senses, Firstspace. This same space as conceived space, Secondspace, would be a photograph or architectural drawing of the space, or your mental picture of what the space will look like after renovation. Thirdspace—a synthesis of these two—addresses how one may experience space. The room you occupy might produce any number of possible responses: a sense of tranquility or oppression; fond memories or unpleasant ones. The point here is that space is never neutral or merely a physical location that can be represented conceptually through a photograph, painting, architectural drawing, or map, as if the representation was a one-to-one likeness of the physical space.

Lefebvre's work on the social production of space has significant implications for the academic study of religion. While sacred space has been studied previously—most notably by Mircea Eliade—such considerations usually take a modernist perspective toward spatiality, positing a universally existing, natural, and largely monolithic notion of the bifurcation of sacred and profane space. Theories of religious space that depart from Eliade's dualistic conceptions remain nascent, though exceptions exist, most notably in the work of Jonathan Z. Smith (see, for instance, *To Take Place: Toward Theory in Ritual*). Most recently, the theories of Lefebvre and Soja have been central to the research and studies produced by the Constructions of Ancient Space Seminar of the Society of Biblical Literature and the American Academy of Religion (see the papers by Boer and Flanagan).

Further Reading

By Lefebvre

***The Production of Space*. Translated by Donald Nicholson-Smith. Oxford: Blackwell, 1991.

***Critique of Everyday Life*. Vol. 1. Translated by John Moore. London: Verso Books, 1991.

Critique of Everyday Life. Vol. 2. Translated by John Moore. London: Verso Books, 2002.

Critique of Everyday Life. Vol. 3, *From Modernity to Modernism (Towards a Metaphilosophy of Daily Life)*. Translated by Gregory Elliott. London: Verso Books, 2003.

Henri Lefebvre: Key Writings. Edited by Stuart Elden, Elizabeth Lebas, and Eleonore Kofman. New York: Continuum, 2003.

About Lefebvre

Boer, Roland. "Sanctuary and Womb: Henri Lefebvre and the Production of Space." Paper presented at the Constructions of Ancient Space Seminar of the Society for Biblical Literature and the American Academy of Religion. 2000. <http://www.cwru.edu/affil/GAIR/papers/2000papers/Boer.html>.

Flanagan, James W. "Ancient Perceptions of Space/Perceptions of Ancient Space." *Semeia* 87 (1999): 15–43.

———. "The Trialectics of Biblical Studies." Paper presented at the Constructions of Ancient Space Seminar of the Society for Biblical Literature and the American Academy of Religion. 2001. <http://www.cwru.edu/affil/GAIR/papers/2001papers/flanagan1.htm>.

Gunn, David M., and Paula M. McNutt, Eds. *Imagining Biblical Worlds: Studies in Spatial, Social and Historical Constructs in Honor of James W. Flanagan*. New York: Continuum, 2003.

Harvey, David. *The Condition of Postmodernity: An Enquiry into the Origins of Cultural Change*. Cambridge, Mass.: Blackwell, 1989.

***Soja, Edward W. *Thirdspace: Journeys to Los Angeles and Other Real-and-Imagined Places*. Malden, Mass.: Blackwell, 1996.

EMMANUEL LEVINAS

Key Concepts

- ethics as first philosophy
- the other (alterity)
- face-to-face
- transcendence

Emmanuel Levinas (1906–1995) was born in Kovno, Lithuania. His parents, devout Jews, were part of a distinguished Jewish community. In 1923 he moved to Strasbourg, where he studied philosophy. In 1928–1929 he studied under the phenomenologist Edmund Husserl in Freiburg. Soon after he discovered the work of Heidegger, whom he would later criticize for his complicity with Nazism. In 1939 he began serving as a translator of German and Russian in the French military but was captured a year later by the Nazis who, on account of his officer's uniform, put him in a prisoner of war camp rather than a concentration camp. He described his life as dominated by the memory of Nazi horror. After the war, he studied Hebrew Scriptures and the Talmud in Paris with the famous Monsieur Chouchani (who was then also teaching the young Holocaust survivor Elie Wiesel, another Lithuanian). In addition to his philosophical works, he wrote a number of important essays on the Talmud.

Levinas served as teacher and director of the Alliance Israelite Universelle until 1961, when he published his doctoral thesis, *Totality and Infinity*, and was appointed professor of philosophy at Poitiers. In 1967 he moved to the University of Paris-Nanterre, and in 1973 he took a position at the Sorbonne (Paris IV), from which he retired in 1976.

For most of Levinas' career he remained a relatively obscure philosopher, known primarily for his interpretations of Husserl and Heidegger (his early work on Husserl influenced Jean-Paul Sartre and Simone de Beauvoir, among others). Attention was drawn to his work in 1964 by Jacques **DERRIDA**'s famous essay on *Totality and Infinity* called "Violence and Metaphysics." Since then, his influence among religionists has grown exponentially. Levinas died in 1995 on December 25—the eighth day of Hanukkah that year.

Central to Levinas's philosophy is the claim that ethics—encapsulated in one's responsibility for and obligation to the other—is the foundation of all philosophy and the heart of human existence. This is what he means in *Totality and Infinity* by "**ethics as first philosophy**." The Oracle at Delphi gave us the philosophical dictum, "know yourself." But Levinas counters that the heart of philosophy is not about knowing and not about oneself alone. The heart of philosophy—the heart of life—is found not in knowing yourself but in your relation to **the other**. The other is essentially the not-me, that which is beyond me, exterior to me, outside the reach of my own system of thought, beyond my own self-understanding and understanding of the world.

In Levinas's writing, the privileged image for one's encounter with the other is the **face-to-face**. The face of the other confronts me in a nonsymmetrical relationship. I am obliged to this other, who implores, "do not kill me." Killing here should be taken both literally and figuratively. One can kill, in Levinas's sense, simply by denying the other's existence or by reducing the other's otherness to oneself, that is, to sameness. When I "make sense" of the other according to my own system of thought, when I explain the other away, or when I regard the other as a means to my own ends, I have killed the other otherness.

For Levinas, then, the face-to-face encounter is an "ultimate situation," for it is "present in its refusal to be contained" (*Totality and Infinity*, p. 81; p. 194). It obliges me to open myself to it, thereby breaking open my own self-contained identity and my own sense of security and at-homeness. By way of example, consider the relationship between Job and his so-called friends in the Book of Job (Beal, "Facing Job"). As readers, we know that Job's intense suffering is entirely undeserved. God is allowing him to suffer precisely because he is so perfectly righteous. Job insists on his innocence—that he is suffering unjustly. For him, his undeserved suffering calls into question his whole religious worldview, according to which the righteous are supposed to prosper and the wicked are supposed to suffer. His "friends," in addition, insist on maintaining that old worldview in the face of Job's suffering. They insist that there is a good reason for his suffering, that his suffering is theologically justified—he deserves it. In so doing, they try to contain his otherness within their traditional religious worldview, thereby reducing his otherness to sense within their system. In God's world, they reason, righteous people prosper and wicked people suffer. Job is suffering, so he must be wicked. Thus they sacrifice Job, as the face of the other, to their established religious worldview. This despite Job's imploring, "Face me, and be appalled. Put your hand over your mouth" (Job 21:5).

For Levinas, the ultimate situation of the face-to-face encounter implies a kind of religious experience, that is, an encounter with **transcendence**, albeit not the kind of religious experience that tends to affirm or shore up the foundations of any religious certainty. Moreover, in one's relation to the individual other person (*Autrui*) in such an encounter, one becomes aware of radical, transcendent otherness, the wholly other (*autre*) or "alterity," which cannot be contained in thought or reduced to a system and is ultimately beyond knowing. In this respect, Levinas describes the individual face of the other as the trace of God, where divine glory is manifest. Thus an encounter with the other person in a relationship of obligation is in the same moment an encounter with transcendence as exteriority, radical otherness. Every face-to-face encounter in daily life is, potentially, a religious experience.

Because of his work in both philosophy and Jewish Scriptures, interest in Levinas's work among religionists has tended to be concentrated in the fields of biblical studies, philosophy of religion, and theological ethics. Beyond these fields, Levinas's work carries great potential for the study of religion. On the one hand, his critique of totalizing systems of thought that "kill" the other by reducing its otherness to itself speaks directly against the project of developing a universal, totalizing theory of religion that can make sense of all the particulars that we think of as "religious." Any theory of religion has a fundamental ethical obligation to the face of the other. On the other hand, Levinas's understanding of one's ethical encounter with the face of the other person as a kind of religious encounter with transcendence might open possibilities toward more constructive theories of religious experience that bridge the chasm between social-scientific and phenomenological approaches to religion. In particular, we note the work of anthropologist of religion Thomas J. Csordas, who has developed a phenomenological theory of religion in terms of the human relation to otherness.

Further Reading

By Levinas

Totality and Infinity: An Essay on Exteriority. Translated by Alfonso Lingis. Pittsburgh: Dusquesne University Press, 1969.

Ethics and Infinity: Conversations with Philippe Nemo. Translated by Richard A. Cohen. Pittsburgh: Dusquesne University Press, 1985.

Nine Talmudic Readings by Emmanuel Levinas. Translated by Annette Aronowicz. Bloomington: Indiana University Press, 1990.

Is It Righteous to Be?: Interviews with Emmanuel Levinas. Edited by Jill Robbins. Stanford: Stanford Univesity Press, 2001.

The Levinas Reader. Edited by Sean Hand. Oxford: Blackwell, 1990.

"Nemo, Philippe. Preface." In *Job and the Excess of Evil*. Translated by Michael Kigel. Pittsburgh: Duquesne University Press, 1998.

About Levinas

Beal, Timothy K. "Facing Job." In *Levinas and Biblical Studies*, edited by Tamara Eskenazi and Gary A. Phillips. Atlanta-Society of Biblical Literature, 2003.

Bloechl, Jeffrey, ed. *The Face of the Other & the Trace of God: Essays on the Philosophy of Emmanuel Levinas*. New York: Fordham University Press, 2000.

Blond, Phillip. "Emmanuel Levinas: God and Phenomenology." In *Post-secular Philosophy: Between Philosophy and Theology*, edited by Phillip Blond. London and New York: Routledge, 1998.

*Cornell, Drucilla. *The Philosophy of the Limit*. New York and London: Routledge, 1992.

Csordas, Thomas J. "Asymptote of the Ineffable: Embodiment, Alterity, and the Theory of Religion." *Current Anthropology* 45 (2004): 163–86.

Derrida, Jacques. *Adieu to Emmanuel Levinas*. Translated by Pascale-Anne Brault and Michael Naas. Stanford: Stanford University Press, 1999.

———. "Violence and Metaphysics: An Essay on the Thought of Emmanuel Levinas." In *Writing and Difference*, translated by Alan Bass. Chicago: University of Chicago Press, 1978.

*Eskenazi, Tamara, and Gary A. Phillips, Eds. Levinas and Biblical Studies. Atlanta-Society of Biblical Literature, 2003.

Kosky, Jeffrey L. *Levinas and the Philosophy of Religion*. Bloomington: Indiana University Press, 2001.

Shapiro, Susan E. "Rhetoric, Ideology, and Idolatry in the Writings of Emmanuel Levinas." In *Rhetorical Invention and Religious Inquiry: New Perspectives*, edited by Walter Jost and Wendy Olmsted. New Haven: Yale University Press, 2000.

Wyschogrod, Edith. "Emmanuel Levinas and Hillel's Questions." In *Postmodern Philosophy and Christian Thought*, edited by Merold Westphal. Bloomington: Indiana University Press, 1999.

JEAN-FRANÇOIS LYOTARD

Key Concepts

- metanarrative
- postmodern condition
- petits récits
- differend
- "Judeo-Christian"
- experience of the sublime

Jean-François Lyotard (1924–1998) studied phenomenology under Maurice **MERLEAU-PONTY**. He began his career as a secondary school teacher in Algeria and later taught philosophy at the University of Paris, from which he retired in 1989. He then went on to visiting professorships at several American universities, including Yale and Emory.

Lyotard demonstrated an interest in religion, especially Judaism, throughout his career. As Robert Woodruff Visiting Professor at Emory, he taught several graduate philosophy seminars in which religious experience was a central theme, including a course on the experience of the sublime in Kant's *Critique of Judgment* and another on the theme of conversion in Georges **BATAILLE**'s *Inner Experience* and Augustine's *Confessions*.

From his earliest work, Lyotard displayed resistance to the so-called structuralist "linguistic turn" that emphasized the way language shapes experience and which was so influential among many of his contemporaries in France in the 1950s and 1960s (e.g., Lévi-Strauss, **LACAN**, **BARTHES**). He insisted that there is always a chasm between experience and language, and that one must not rule out extralinguistic experience. Language, he insisted, does not construct our lifeworld completely; there are experiences that language does not and cannot present.

Lyotard's two most influential works are *The Postmodern Condition* (1979), originally written as a report on the current state of knowledge for the government of Quebec, and *The Differend* (1983). The two are closely related and together provide a valuable introduction to Lyotard's philosophy.

A key concept in *The Postmodern Condition* is "**metanarrative**," or "master narrative." Lyotard uses this term to refer to the overarching mythic narratives that individuals and societies tell in order to situate their particular time and place within the context of a larger story, thereby giving it broader significance. A metanarrative locates a current situation, whether individual or communal, within a larger narrative structure that plots movement toward some ultimate objective—progress, triumph of reason, victory of the proletariat, redemption.

The "**postmodern condition**"—ascribed to the contemporary West—is one in which there is an increasing "incredulity" and distrust toward metanarratives. Lyotard argues that metanarratives are being replaced by a proliferation of *petits récits*, "little stories" or testimonies that draw attention to particulars as opposed to universals, that is, to local events, individual experiences, heterodox ideas, and other practices and narratives that do not fit within a larger, universal metanarrative. Within the postmodern condition there is a newfound interest in the particular differences and dissensions that challenge the drive toward homogeneity and oneness, a drive which is propelled by a totalizing metanarrative that Lyotard describes as "totalitarian." Against this drive, Lyotard urges us to "wage war on totality; let us be witness to the unpresentable; let us activate the differences and save the honor of the name" (*The Postmodern Condition*, p. 82).

Lyotard continues this line of thought, including its ethical imperative to activate particular differences against totalizing universals, in *The Differend*. Here, Lyotard uses the term "**differend**" to explain the silencing of particular differences that do not fit within larger conceptual or social totalities. It is the sign that someone or something has been denied voice or visibility because it has been viewed by the dominant ideological system as unacceptable. Such radical differences are suppressed because they cannot be subsumed under larger, "universal" concepts without doing violence to them. "Differend" means at once dispute, difference, and otherness (alterity).

In this regard, Lyotard was particularly interested in how the Jews and their history are marginalized within the largely Christian metanarrative of Western culture. The most extreme instance of this may be found in the "forgetting" of the Holocaust, an event that radically undermines the Western myth of progress and humanism. In *Heidegger and "the jews"* (first published in French in 1988), for example, he explores the irony that Heidegger, the great philosopher of forgotten Being, has more or less willfully forgotten the Holocaust and the Jews. We must always remember that something has been forgotten that must not be forgotten, and that our very lives are indebted to that something. This was, for Lyotard, Heidegger's sin.

Along similar lines, one of Lyotard's last works, *Hyphen* (first published in French in 1993), argues that the hyphen in "**Judeo-Christian**" marks the subsumption of Judaism within Christianity. While appearing to embrace and identify with Judaism, the idea of the Judeo-Christian in fact erases Judaism's actual difference and dissension within the predominantly Christian West.

Another sign of the differend that interested Lyotard was the **experience of the sublime**, which is, in Rudolph Otto's *The Idea of the Holy* and elsewhere, likened to religious experience as an encounter with radical otherness that is beyond accountability by the faculties of reason or imagination and that elicits both fascination and dread. In *Heidegger and "the jews,"* and in *Analytic of the Sublime* (first published in French in 1991), and in lectures given toward the end of his life at Emory University, Lyotard describes the experience of the sublime in terms of an "anaesthetics" of overwhelming shock and stupefaction, suspending one in an irreducible tension of wonder and terror. In his work on the experience of the sublime, we can clearly see Lyotard's orientation toward the idea that experience is beyond language and that unpresentables exist.

Lyotard's analysis of how metanarratives operate in Western culture has interesting ramifications for religious studies. Many would argue that the academic study of religion is at heart the quest for a metanarrative of the history of religions. Early theories of religion such as those of E. B. Tylor and James Frazer were essentially metanarratives of the development of human consciousness as it progresses from "primitive" (non-Western) to "modern" (Western). Similarly, Durkheim viewed religion as that which pertains to the whole (identified with the sacred) over against the particular (identified with the profane). The turn in religious studies toward examination of particular, local religious discourses and practices may be understood as a response to the critique by Lyotard and others of the modernist orientation toward totalizing metanarratives that privilege the universal at the expense of the particular. Such approaches are indeed *petits récits*.

Lyotard's work raises one especially important question for students of religion: is it possible to construct a theory of religion that does not reduce or erase that which it cannot make sense of or present? Can any theory of religion remain open to the "unpresentable" and the "forgotten," to that which it cannot accommodate?

Further Reading

By Lyotard

The Differend: Phrases in Dispute. Translated by Georges Van Den Abbeele. Minneapolis: University of Minnesota Press, 1989.

*Heidegger and "the jews." Translated by Andreas Michel and Mark S. Roberts. Minneapolis: University of Minnesota Press, 1990.

The Postmodern Condition: A Report on Knowledge. Translated by Geoff Bennington and Brian Massumi. Minneapolis: University of Minnesota Press, 1984.

Hyphen: Between Judaism and Christianity. Translated by Pascale-Anne Brault and Michael Naas. Humanity Books, 1999.

Lessons on the Analytic of the Sublime: Kant's Critique of Judgment. Translated by Elizabeth Rottenberg Stanford: Stanford University Press, 1994.

About Lyotard

Boeve, Lieven. "J-F Lyotard's Critique of Master Narratives: Towards a Postmodern Political Theology." In *Liberation Theologies on Shifting Grounds*, edited by G. De Schrijver. Louvain: Leuven University Press, 1998.

Cox, James L. "Religious Typologies and the Postmodern Critique." *Method & Theory in the Study of Religion* 10 (1998): 244–62.

*Crockett, Clayton. *A Theology of the Sublime.* New York and London: Routledge, 2001.

Macquarrie, John. "Postmodernism in Philosophy of Religion and Theology." *International Journal for Philosophy of Religion* 50 (2001): 9–27.

Taylor, Victor E. *Para/Inquiry: Postmodern Religion and Culture.* New York and London: Routledge, 1999.

Westphal, Merold. "Postmodernism and the Gospel: Onto-Theology, Metanarratives, and Perspectivism." *Perspectives* 15 (2000): 6–10.

MAURICE MERLEAU-PONTY

Key Concepts

- primacy of perception
- lived experience
- lived body
- embodiment
- body-subject

Maurice Merleau-Ponty (1908–61) was a French intellectual particularly interested in the nature of human consciousness as embodied experience. He was born in Rochefort-sur-mer, France. As a student at the the the École normale supérieure, he became interested in phenomenology—the philosophical study of the perception of things—through the work of Husserl and Heidegger. After graduating in 1930, Merleau-Ponty taught at different high schools. During the 1930s he was associated with the leftist Catholic journal, *Esprit*.

Merleau-Ponty served as an officer in the French army at the beginning of World War II. During the German occupation, while participating in the French resistance, he taught in Paris and composed *The Phenomenology of Perception* (first published in French in 1945), widely regarded as his most important work. Following the war, he co-founded the existentialist journal, *Les Temps Modernes*, along with Jean-Paul Sartre and Simone de Beauvoir. In 1952, after repeated political disagreements with Sartre over the latter's support of North Korea during the Korean War, Merleau-Ponty resigned from the journal's editorial board. Merleau-Ponty's postwar academic career included academic positions at the Sorbonne and, from 1952 until his death, at the Collège de France.

Merleau-Ponty's thought centers on understanding the lived, embodied nature of human consciousness and perception. Among noted theorists influenced by Merleau-Ponty's work were Claude Lévi-Strauss, Michel **FOUCAULT**, Paul Ricoeur, and Louis **ALTHUSSER**. More recently, Merleau-Ponty's work has been pursued by social scientists interested in critiquing traditional assumptions about the relationship between body and mind and the nature of human experience. He has also influenced religion scholars interested in understanding religious experience as embodied perception (for instance, anthropologist of religion Thomas Csordas's studies of religious healing, see *Body/ Meaning/ Healing* and *The Sacred Self*).

In order to understand Merleau-Ponty's philosophical views, we need to briefly consider phenomenology, a perspective that informs much of his thinking. As the name suggests, phenomenology explores phenomena—anything perceived directly by the senses. The German founder of phenomenology, Edmund Husserl, argues that although philosophical proofs for the independent existence of objects perceived through the senses are impossibly difficult to establish, human beings nevertheless experience the external world as objects of consciousness, regardless of the ultimate ontological status of these things. Husserl says that we need to "bracket off" concern over proofs and other questions for which definitive answers are not readily forthcoming. Instead, he says, we should concentrate on investigating the sensual perceptions that constitute our experiences of ideas, images, emotions, objects, and other things that are perceived through consciousness. The main concern, however, is with the experience of these objects that engage our attention, not with an analysis of their status independent of our consciousness. Thus Husserl established phenomenology as the analysis of experiences that result from consciousness of external objects.

Merleau-Ponty's intellectual contributions are, in part, extensions of Husserl's version of phenomenology and center on the concepts of embodiment and perception. These ideas are explored in *Phenomenology of Perception*. Here Merleau-Ponty critiques the Cartesian body/mind dichotomy by arguing for the collapse of this dualistic way of understanding human beings existing in the world. He emphasizes the necessity to recognize that people are not simply—or primarily—disembodied thinking minds, but rather bodies connected to a material world. Bodies are, therefore, not something abstract, but rather concrete entities in the world through which perception occurs and subjectivity is formed. For Merleau-Ponty, the world is the ground of experience. Any subjectivity is of the world, not separate or disconnected from it, and is fueled by what he terms the "**primacy of perception**." Our access to the world is through the body, not through, or only through, the mind. Contrary to Descartes' dictum, *Cogito ergo sum* ("I think, therefore I am"), existence is not thinking but embodiment. Indeed, all thinking is embodied; it derives from consciousness, which itself develops from the subject's bodily perceptions. These perceptions undergird rationalization and other conscious and logical operations on their meaning.

In the Husserlian view (itself indebted to Cartesian philosophy), human beings are entities centered on consciousness. Against this view, Merleau-Ponty insists that human identity—our subjectivity—is informed significantly by our physicality, our bodies. He therefore asserts the centrality of the body and the body's influence on our perception of the experienced world. Knowledge of the world, he says, derives from concrete perception, not from abstract thought or the workings of a disembodied mind or consciousness. In short, he prioritizes the body over the mind in our experience of the world. Perception itself is incarnate: perceptions do not exist as bodiless abstractions but rather within bodies. Perception only occurs in the world of lived experience. Perception does not exist as an abstraction transcending or standing outside of the lived body.

Merleau-Ponty asserted that it is through **lived experience** that we gain knowledge of the world. He states that the activities of the body in the world constitute lived experience. Such experience is never fixed but is always in process. We both shape and are shaped by our lived experiences. The mind that perceives things is incarnate in the body. Perception and consciousness are not separate from or transcendent of lived experience in the world.

Perception is directly connected to the **lived body**. By lived body, Merleau-Ponty is referring to both the body that experiences the world and the body that is experienced. The subject (person) doing the perceiving is embodied. This embodiment is thus the link to the external, phenomenal, experienced world. Humans consist of conscious components, but it is our bodily aspects that determine who we are. Despite the insistence by some influential philosophers that consciousness is foundational to what it means to be a human being, Merleau-Ponty argues that whatever we experience in the world or understand about the world derives fundamentally from our bodies and our embodied minds. Perception underpins categorization or theorization even if it appears that we have thoughts and conceptualizations about the world that we only secondarily experience physically. The world can only be viewed from our physical time and place. As Merleau-Ponty states: "Our own body is in the world as the heart is in the organism: it keeps the visible spectacle constantly alive, it breathes life into it and sustains it inwardly, and with it forms a system" (*Phenomenology of Perception,* p. 235).

A key idea expressed in Merleau-Ponty's work is the notion of **embodiment**. According to Merleau-Ponty, it is not just the mind that perceives, experiences, and represents the world—a traditional philosophical view of the centrality of mind. Instead, the concept of embodiment asserts that the body plays a central role in how one experiences the world. As Merleau-Ponty understands it, the world is not an external object to think about, but rather is the ground for our perceptions and experiences. Thus the external things we perceive as objects in the world are the result of how our bodies experience them, not simply the product of consciousness recognizing the object. Philosophical ideas that consciousness does all the work of perceiving the world are erroneous.

From Merleau-Ponty's perspective, you cannot have consciousness without the body—body and mind are inextricably bound. Subjectivity, then, is incarnate. For Merleau-Ponty, embodied knowledge precludes the possibility of a realm of autonomous knowledge gained prior to or without the body. Analysis of the world is always the activity of an embodied mind.

The concept of **body-subject** is used by Merleau-Ponty in *Phenomenology of Perception* to refer to the idea that the body, mind, and world are completely intertwined and not separable as Cartesian thought asserts. Merleau-Ponty's phenomenology seeks to understand this interconnection, not to try to locate some immutable consciousness transcending the world as experienced by bodies. The notion of body-subject underscores Merleau-Ponty's insistence that it is a body that connects a person to the world. Cartesian duality breaks down at this juncture. There is no disembodied mind that observes objects out there in the world. We live in the world by way of our bodies. Subject and object are a unity, not a duality. That is, you must not treat them as separate realms, but rather as two sides of the same entity that exists—embodied—in the world.

Books, articles, conferences, and courses on religion and the body have become quite widespread. Merleau-Ponty's ideas on the primacy of perception are only now beginning to be used to think about religion as something experienced physically—through the body. Western perspectives on religion, embedded in a Cartesian paradigm, have tended to understand religion as having primarily to do with what one believes—the conscious mind. Though there are obvious exceptions, bodies have usually been seen as deleterious to the achievement of spiritual aspirations. Religious asceticism is one example of practices to discipline the body so that the real work of religion occurring in the mind can proceed unhindered. Merleau-Ponty's theory offers a significant alternative to traditional views.

Further Reading

By Merleau-Ponty

Phenomenology of Perception. 2nd ed. Translated by Colin Smith. London and New York: Routledge, 2002.

The Structure of Behavior. Translated by Alden L. Fisher. Boston: Beacon Press, 1963.

The Visible and the Invisible. Edited by Claude Lefort and translated by Alphonso Lingis. Evanston: Northwestern University Press, 1968.

The Primacy of Perception. Translated by James M. Edie. Evanston, IL.: Northwestern University Press, 1964.

The Essential Writings of Merleau-Ponty. Edited by Alden L. Fisher. New York: Harcourt, Brace and World, 1969.

About Merleau-Ponty

Barral, Mary Rose. *Merleau-Ponty: The Role of the Body-Subject in Interpersonal Relations.* Pittsburgh: Duquesne University Press, 1965.

Csordas, Thomas J. *The Sacred Self: A Cultural Phenomenology of Charismatic Healing.* Berkeley: University of California Press, 1997.

————. *Body/Meaning/Healing.* New York: Palgrave, 2000.

Dillon, M. C. *Merleau-Ponty's Ontology.* 2nd ed. Evanston: Northwestern University Press, 1997.

Evans, Fred, and Leonard Lawlor, eds. *Chiasms: Merleau-Ponty's Notion of Flesh.* Albany: State University of New York Press, 2000.

Langer, Monika M. *Merleau-Ponty's Phenomenology of Perception: A Guide and Commentary.* Tallahassee: Florida State University Press, 1989.

*Priest, Stephen. *Merleau-Ponty.* London and New York: Routledge, 1998.

Primozic, Daniel Thomas. *On Merleau-Ponty.* Belmont, CA: Wadsworth, 2001.

Wyschogrod, Edith. *Saints and Postmodernism: Revisioning Moral Philosophy.* Chicago: University of Chicago Press, 1990.

EDWARD W. SAID

Key Concepts

- postcolonial criticism
- colonial discourse
- Orientalism
- imperialism
- contrapuntal reading

Edward W. Said (1935–2003) was a postcolonial literary critic and the Parr Professor of English and Comparative Literature at Columbia University. Born in Jerusalem in 1935, Said's Palestinian family became refugees in 1948 and moved to Egypt, where he attended British schools. He also spent time during his youth in Lebanon and Jordan before immigrating to the United States. He earned his B.A. from Princeton University in 1957 and his Ph.D. in literature from Harvard University in 1964. He spent his entire academic career as a professor of English and comparative literature at Columbia University. He died in 2003 after a long battle with leukemia.

Said's work included both intellectual and political pursuits. On the one hand, he is well known for his engagements with literary criticism and postcolonial theory, often drawing from theoretical perspectives and methods developed by Michel **FOUCAULT**. On the other hand, he was politically active as an advocate of Palestinian independence and human rights. Critical of U.S. foreign policy, especially in the Middle East, he also spoke out against corruption within Palestine.

Said's intellectual and political agendas address the ways in which white Europeans and North Americans fail to understand—or even try to understand— differences between Western culture and non-Western cultures. His studies on Orientalism expressly address this complex of issues. This work has arguably the deepest resonance for religious studies, especially for those dealing with non-Western religions or for those involved in research on Western views of non-Western religions. The history of Christian missionary activity, for instance, is largely implicated in Said's critique.

Said's **postcolonial criticism** is particularly concerned with issues of discourse and representation in relation to the history of Western colonialism. Said asks questions about how colonized cultures are represented, about the power of these representations to shape and control other cultures, and about **colonial discourse**, that is, the discourse through which colonizer/colonized subject positions are constructed.

Following Foucault, Said understands discourse as systems of linguistic usage and codes—discursive formations, whether written or spoken—that produce knowledge and practice about particular conceptual fields, demarcating what can be known, said, or enacted in relation to this body of knowledge. Thus, for example, medical discourse establishes knowledge about such things as the hierarchical nature of the doctor-patient relationship, the identification and classification of diseases, and distinctions between physical and mental illness. It is through different discourses that we know about and categorize the world. For Foucault, there are significant ramifications to the discursive process. In any cultural setting, there are dominant groups that establish what can and cannot be said and done by others on the basis of the discursive knowledge they impose on others—the dominated. In the end, both dominant and dominated are made into subjects of this knowledge and live within the parameters that the discursive knowledge allows. This knowledge attains the status or appearance of an independent reality, and its origins as a social construction are forgotten. Discursive knowledge is also invariably connected to power. Those in control of a particular discourse have control over what can be known and, hence, have power over others.

Discourse, as a form of knowledge that exerts power, is of particular importance in Said's articulation of the nature of **Orientalism**, Western discourse about the East that engenders the oppressor-oppressed relationship pertaining between colonizer and colonized (see especially *Orientalism* and *Culture and Imperialism*). Said focuses on the ways in which discursive formations about the "Orient" exert power and control over those subjected to them. For Said, the concept of Orientalism has three dimensions: the discursive, the academic, and the imaginative. All three, though, are interconnected and should be understood as such. The *discursive* concerns the notion that "Orientalism can be discussed and analyzed as the corporate institution for dealing with the Orient—dealing with it by making statements about it, authorizing views of it, describing it, by teaching it, settling it, ruling over it: in short, Orientalism as a Western style for dominating, restructuring, and having authority over the Orient" (*Orientalism*, p. 3). The *academic* refers to the idea that "[a]nyone who teaches, writes about, or researches the Orient—and this applies whether the person is an anthropologist, sociologist, historian, or philologist—either in its specific or its general aspects, is an Orientalist, and what he or she does is Orientalism" (*Orientalism*, p. 2). Finally, the *imaginative* refers to the idea that

"Orientalism is a style of thought based upon an ontological and epistemological distinction made between 'the Orient' and (most of the time) 'the Occident'" (*Orientalism* 2). Said refers to this culturally constructed space as an "imaginative geography" (*Orientalism*, p. 54).

Orientalism (1978), Said's groundbreaking study that explores the intellectual history of European (particularly British and French) representations of the Arab Middle East, is an early example of postcolonial criticism. Indeed, Said's work on Orientalism cannot be understood without framing it within the larger concept of postcolonialism and the postcolonial theory that examines it. Postcolonial theory and criticism, which became prominent in the 1990s, are concerned with analyzing the relationship between culture and colonial power, exploring the cultural products of societies that were once under colonial rule. Postcolonial Indian and African literature, for instance, addresses such issues as the lingering effects of colonialism on identity, nationality, and the nature of resistance to colonial power.

One goal of postcolonial theory is to question universal, humanist claims that cultural products can contain timeless and culturally transcendent ideas and values. When, for instance, colonizing nations make universal claims—claiming to make judgments on the basis of some universal standard—the colonized, other culture is by default seen as tentative and provisional. These other cultures are somehow "less than" the colonial power. Victorian British literature often claims to represent the universal human condition. In so doing, Indian culture is seen—whether consciously or unconsciously—as misrepresenting the truth or reality discoverable in the world by those with the ability to do so. Postcolonial theory refutes this universalist impulse and instead seeks to give voice to local practices, ideas, and values. Eurocentrism, which places Europe at the center and relegates non-European culture to the margins, is seen as a hegemonic power that must be resisted. A problematic side effect of colonialism is that in a postcolonial culture people have to locate strategies for reclaiming their cultural past and prizing its value.

The nature of colonial discourse and the ways in which it was used to wield power and control over the colonized is therefore central to Said's thesis in *Orientalism*. This volume explicates ways in which Western colonizers constructed the colonized as "other." Ways in which colonizers represented the colonized also created a social hierarchy and hegemonic power over the colonized. Said's analysis focuses especially on the Middle East as "Orient," but his thesis can be extended to other cultural contexts where colonization occurred (and is still occurring).

Said critiques Eurocentric universalism for its setting up a binary opposition of the superiority of Western cultures and the inferiority of colonized, non-Western cultures. Said identifies this perspective as a central aspect of "Orientalism." This view sees the Middle East—and by extension, Africa, South and Southeast Asia, and East Asia—as the "Orient," an "other" inferior to Western culture. Said points out that Orientalist discourse has the pernicious effect of treating the colonized as if they were all the same. Thus "Orientals" are perceived not as freely choosing, autonomous individuals, but rather as homogeneous, faceless peoples who are known by their commonality of values, emotions, and personality traits. They are, in effect, essentialized to a few stereotypical—and often negative—characteristics and rendered as lacking individual personalities. A strong racist tendency is also operating in such views. Said provides numerous accounts of colonial administrators and travelers who describe and represent Arabs in dehumanizing ways. After citing one such example he remarks: "In such statements as these, we note immediately that 'the Arab' or 'Arabs' have an aura of apartness, definiteness, and collective self-consistency such as to wipe out any traces of individual Arabs with narratable life histories" (*Orientalism*, p. 229).

Orientalist discourse, says Said, makes possible "the enormous systematic discipline by which European culture was able to manage—and even produce—the Orient politically, sociologically, militarily, ideologically, scientifically, and imaginatively during the post-Enlightenment period" (*Orientalism*, p. 3). Said is less interested in refuting some notion that this discourse is "true" in some essential, transcendent way than with marking out the ground by which colonial discourse acted on the objects of its knowledge claims. Said asserts: "The Orient was almost a European invention, and had been since antiquity a place of romance, exotic beings, haunting memories and landscapes, remarkable experiences" (*Orientalism*, p. 1). For Said, the issue is not whether this European representation is true, but rather what are the effects of this representation in the world.

If colonial discourse oppressed the colonized subject, it also worked its effects on those who wielded this language in the first place. For Said, Orientalism delineates a relationship between "Europe" and the "Orient." For instance, the concept of "the Orient has helped to define Europe (or the West) as its contrasting image, idea, personality, experience'" (*Orientalism*, pp. 1–2). Thus European identity is framed in terms of what it is or—more likely—is not in relation to a constructed "Orient." Concepts of the Orient also create a self-identity for Europe. "Europe" is as much a fiction as is the Orient if by "Europe" we mean some homogenous entity that is known by a set of essential "European" characteristics.

In a later study, *Culture and Imperialism*, Said draws a distinction between **imperialism** and colonialism. For Said, "'imperialism' means the practice, the theory, and the attitudes of a dominating metropolitan center ruling a distant territory; 'colonialism,' which is almost always a consequence of imperialism, is the implanting of settlements on distant territory" (*Culture and Imperialism*, p. 9). Imperialism is embedded in colonial discourse and serves as an important tool for creating the colonized subject. Said argues that any discourse that comments on a colonized culture cannot remain neutral or stand outside a consideration of imperialism because all such discourses are invested in how the view of the other is constructed. One need only consult the literature, history, and other cultural products of a colonizing nation that are directed at the colonized to find, for instance, the colonized equated with the "other."

The history of colonialism and Orientalism is deeply entangled with the history of religion in the West, and Said has been extremely important to efforts to draw attention to this fact within the field of religious studies (see, for instance King, *Orientalism and Religion*; Moore, "Postcolonialism"; and Sugirtharajah, *The Bible and the Third World*). How might one tease out from a religious text those aspects of colonial discourse that may be embedded therein? Said's notion of **contrapuntal reading** is particularly suggestive. Borrowing the concept of counterpoint from music, Said (who also wrote on music) describes a strategy for reading that exposes the colonial discourses hidden within a text. Contrapuntal reading not only unveils the colonial perspective, but it also tries to read for nuances of resistance (counterpoints) that may also be lurking within the narrative. Said argues that we need to "read the great canonical texts, and perhaps the entire archive of modern and pre-modern European and American culture, with an effort to draw out, extend, give emphasis and voice to what is silent or marginally present or ideologically represented" (*Culture and Imperialism*, p. 66). In practice, says Said, reading contrapuntally "means reading a text with an understanding of what is involved when an author shows, for instance, that a colonial sugar plantation is seen as important to the process of maintaining a particular style of life in England" (*Culture and Imperialism*, p. 66).

Viewed from a postcolonial perspective, much of the scholarship produced during the nineteenth and twentieth centuries in the discipline that has come to be known as the history of religions participates, whether consciously or not, in colonialist attitudes and practices. For instance, nineteenth-century ethnographers, folklorists, missionaries, and anthropologists have left us with a rich and varied record of their observations of non-Western religions. Among these accounts are descriptions that construct non-Western—particularly non-Christian—religions as "other" by setting them apart as strangely different from "us." Other accounts seek to naturalize and contain these other religions by showing how they are like us in essence, even if their outward practices are clearly different and "exotic." (See Lopez, "Belief," and Smith, "Religion, Religions, Religious" for historical examples of inclusive and exclusive attitudes toward the "other.")

Further Reading

By Said

Orientalism. New York: Pantheon, 1978.

The World, the Text, and the Critic. Cambridge: Harvard University Press, 1983.

Culture and Imperialism. New York: Alfred A. Knopf, 1993.

About Said

*Ashcroft, Bill, and Pal Ahluwalia. *Edward Said*. London and New York: Routledge, 2001.

Chidester, David. "Colonialism." In *Guide to the Study of Religion*, edited by Willi Braun and Russell T. McCutcheon. London and New York: Cassell, 2000.

Hart, William D. *Edward Said and the Religious Effects of Culture*. Cambridge: Cambridge University Press, 2000.

King, Richard. *Orientalism and Religion: Postcolonial Theory, India and "The Mystic East."* London and New York: Routledge, 1999.

Lopez, Donald S., Jr. "Belief." In *Critical Terms for Religious Studies*, edited by Mark C. Taylor. Chicago: University of Chicago Press, 1998.

Lopez, Donald S., Jr., ed. *Curators of the Buddha: The Study of Buddhism under Colonialism*. Chicago: University of Chicago Press, 1995.

Moore, Stephen D. "Postcolonialism." In *Handbook of Postmodern Biblical Interpretation*, edited by A. K. M. Adam. St. Louis: Chalice Press, 2000.

Smith, Jonathan Z. "Religion, Religions, Religious." In *Critical Terms for Religious Studies*, edited by Mark C. Taylor. Chicago: University of Chicago Press, 1998.

Sugirtharajah, R. S. *The Bible and the Third World: Precolonial, Colonial and Postcolonial Encounters*. Cambridge: Cambridge University Press, 2001.

GAYATRI CHAKRAVORTY SPIVAK

Key Concepts

- the subaltern
- othering
- worlding
- strategic essentialism

Gayatri Chakravorty Spivak (1942–) is a Bengali cultural and literary critic. Born in Calcutta, India, to a middle-class family during the waning years of British colonial rule, she attended Presidency College of the University of Calcutta, graduating in 1959 with a degree in English literature. She came to the United States in 1962 and attended graduate school at Cornell University, where she received her Ph.D. in comparative literature under the direction of Paul de Man, who introduced her to the work of Jacques **DERRIDA**. Her 1977 translation of Derrida's *Of Grammatology* (1967) into English made Derrida's work available to a wider audience. She gained initial notoriety from her outstanding introduction to that work, quickly becoming recognized among English-speaking academics seeking help in understanding Derrida's text. Spivak is currently Avalon Foundation Professor in the Humanities at Columbia University.

Spivak operates at the intersections of postcolonial theory, feminism, deconstruction, and Marxism. She rigorously interrogates the binary oppositions that animate both postcolonial and feminist discourse. She further questions concepts found in the imperialist language of colonizers, including concepts of nationhood, fixed identity, and the Third World. The numerous articles and interviews that constitute Spivak's scholarly production have been compiled into several books. *In Other Worlds: Essays in Cultural Politics* (1987) is a collection of essays on a wide range of topics, from Virginia Woolf's *To the Lighthouse*, to French feminism, to the concept of "value." *The Post-Colonial Critic: Interviews, Strategies, Dialogues* (1990) is a compilation of interviews that present Spivak's often difficult thinking in a more reader-friendly format. *Outside in the Teaching Machine* (1993) brings together Spivak's writings on higher education and globalization. *A Critique of Postcolonial Reason: Toward a History of the Vanishing Present* (1999) both expands on her studies of the postcolonial—she explores, for instance, the idea of the "native informant"— and reconsiders and revises some of her earlier work.

Fundamental to Spivak's work is the concept of the **subaltern**. Subaltern means "of inferior rank." Spivak borrows the term from Antonio Gramsci, who used it to refer to social groups under the hegemonic control of the ruling elite. In this sense, the term can refer to any group that is collectively subordinated or disenfranchised, whether on the basis of race, ethnicity, sex, religion, or any other category of identity. Spivak, however, uses this term specifically to refer to the colonized and peripheral subject, especially with reference to those oppressed by British colonialism, such as segments of the Indian population prior to independence. Spivak emphasizes the fact that the female subaltern subject is even more peripheral and marginalized than the male. In the essay, "Can the Subaltern Speak?" (first published in 1985), Spivak observes: "If in the context of colonial production, the subaltern has no history, and cannot speak, the subaltern as female is even more deeply in shadow" ("Can the Subaltern Speak?" p. 28). Spivak's notion of the subaltern is thus also implicated in feminist concerns. She discusses ways that colonialism—and its patriarchy— silences subaltern voices to the extent that they have no conceptual space from which they can speak and be heard, unless, perhaps, they assume the discourse of the oppressing colonizer. The original version of "Can the Subaltern Speak?" discussed here has been enormously influential in postcolonial theoretical circles, but we should note that Spivak revised aspects of her theory of the subaltern in her 1999 book, *A Critique of Postcolonial Reason: Toward a History of the Vanishing Present* (see especially. pp. 306–11).

Another aspect of Western colonialism explored by Spivak is the way that colonial discourse participates in a process she refers to as **othering**. Othering— a term derived from a whole corpus of texts by Hegel, Lacan, Sartre, and others—is an ideological process that isolates groups that are seen as different from the norm of the colonizers. For Spivak, othering is the way in which imperial discourse creates colonized, subaltern subjects. Like Edward **SAID**, she views othering dialectically: the colonizing subject is created in the same moment as the subaltern subject. In this sense, othering expresses a hierarchical, unequal relationship. In her research into this process, Spivak utilizes British colonial office dispatches to reveal othering in historical context. Yet she makes clear that othering is embedded in the discourse of various forms of colonial narrative, fiction as well as nonfiction.

Spivak's concept of **worlding**, derived from Heidegger, is closely related to the dynamics of othering in colonial discourse. Worlding is the process whereby a colonized space is made present in and present to a world crafted by colonial discourse. She states: "If . . . we concentrated on documenting and theorizing the itinerary of the consolidation of Europe as sovereign subject, indeed sovereign and subject, then we would produce an alternative historical narrative of the 'worlding' of what is today called 'the Third World'" ("The Rani of Sirmur," p. 247). A worlding narrative of a colonized space operates to inscribe colonial discourse and hegemony on that space. This is a social construct because it is a "worlding of the world on uninscribed earth" ("The Rani of Sirmur," p. 253). A central way in which the practice of worlding occurs is through mapmaking, but there are ideological aspects as well. For instance, Spivak cites the example of an early nineteenth-century British soldier traveling across India, surveying the land and people: "He is actually engaged in consolidating the self of Europe by obliging the native to cathect the space of the Other on his home ground. He is worlding *their own world*, which is far from mere uninscribed earth, anew, by obliging *them* to domesticate the alien as Master" ("The Rani of Sirmur," p. 253). In effect, the colonized are made to experience their own land as belonging to the colonizer. Worlding and othering, then, are not simply carried out as matters of impersonal national policy, but are enacted by colonizers in local ways, such as the soldier traveling through the countryside.

Spivak often makes reference to the highly problematic nature of terms like "Third World," "Orient," and "Indian." For her, as for Said, these terms are essentialist categories whose meanings hinge on binary oppositions that are of dubious usefulness because of their history and arbitrary nature. Essentialist perspectives stress the idea that conceptual categories name eternal, unchangeable characteristics or identities really existing in the external world. Hence, a category like "Orient" becomes essentialist when it is seen as naming a real place inhabited by people with the same characteristics and personality traits that are eternal and unchanging, and, by extension, inescapable because they are "naturally" possessed. Classic essentialist categories include masculine/feminine and civilized/uncivilized. But essentialist categories are unstable because they are social constructions, not universal names for "real" entities in the world. Further, the categories Spivak discusses were constructed by a colonial discourse whose usage had significant hegemonic and ideological implications and effects. A label like "savage Indian" literally "others" its subject. That is, it forces the colonized into a subaltern subject position not of their own choosing. Once located in a particular subject position, the colonizing power can treat them accordingly, and the subjects often assume this role.

In her 1985 essay, "Subaltern Studies: Deconstructing Historiography," Spivak argues that although essentialism is highly problematic for the knowledge it creates about an "other," there is sometimes a political and social need for what she calls **strategic essentialism**. By this she means a *"strategic* use of positivist essentialism in a scrupulously visible political interest" ("Subaltern Studies: Deconstructing Historiography," p. 205). She argues that it is necessary to assume an essentialist stand—for instance, speaking as a woman or speaking as an Asian—so that the hegemony of patriarchal colonial discourse can be disrupted and questioned. Spivak acknowledges that the application of essentialist categories can have a salutary effect on struggles against oppression and hegemonic power despite the problems inherent in essentialist discourse: "I think it's absolutely on target to take a stand against the discourses of essentialism . . . [b]ut *strategically* we cannot" ("Criticism, Feminism, and The Institution," p. 11). Spivak is arguing that strategic essentialism is expedient, if only in the short term, because it can aid in the process of revitalizing the sense of personal and cultural worth and value of the dominated. One example of this is when postcolonial cultures essentialize their precolonial past in order to find a usable cultural identity.

The intersection of theory and social activism is a tension that runs throughout Spivak's work. For instance, she has been critiqued for her view of strategic essentialism on the grounds that she has given into the very essentialist, universalist language to which she seems to be so adamantly opposed. But for Spivak, the strategic use of essentialist categories is not a matter of violating some notion of theoretical "purity" but rather is necessary from the perspective of social and political exigencies—and identity politics—that require, among other things, certain kinds of discursive tools in order to counter oppression and other ills. Spivak is also critical of Western feminists for sometimes ignoring the plight of women of color and, contrarily, for sometimes presuming to speak for non-Western women on issues about which Western feminists have no direct knowledge or experience. In this latter instance, speaking for non-Western women is to mute once again the voices of women that Western feminists are trying to assist. Such Western feminist discourse creates non-Western women as subaltern subjects and subverts their attempts to speak for themselves.

Spivak's work raises serious questions and issues that have significance for the study of religion. She calls our attention to the need to include the subaltern, especially subaltern women, in our studies of colonial and post-colonial religion. Her work also challenges us to consider how our historical and other studies of, for instance, Indian religion, may unknowingly participate in hegemonic, oppressive practices. Just as Spivak goes back to colonial archives to reanimate silenced voices, so we might return to our own archives of research in order to draw out the beliefs and practices of those who have been disregarded or ignored by historians of religion. Whose story is getting told? Whose story is not? And whose story has been so obscured that it is unrecoverable?

Further Reading

By Spivak

*"The Rani of Sirmur: An Essay in Reading the Archives." *History and Theory* 24 (1985): 247–72.

"Three Women's Texts and a Critique of Imperialism." *Critical Inquiry* 12 (1985): 243–61.

"Subaltern Studies: Deconstructing Historiography." In *In Other Worlds: Essays in Cultural Politics.* New York: Methuen, 1987.

In Other Worlds: Essays in Cultural Politics. New York: Methuen, 1987.

*"Can the Subaltern Speak?" In *The Post-Colonial Studies Reader*, edited by Bill Ashcroft, Gareth Griffiths, and Helen Tiffin. London and New York: Routledge, 1995.

"Criticism, Feminism, and the Institution." In *The Post-Colonial Critic: Interviews, Strategies, Dialogues*, edited by Sarah Harasym. New York and London: Routledge, 1990.

Outside in the Teaching Machine. London and New York: Routledge, 1993.

The Spivak Reader: Selected Works of Gayatri Chakravorty Spivak. Edited by Donna Landry and Gerald MacLean. New York and London: Routledge, 1996.

A Critique of Postcolonial Reason: Toward a History of the Vanishing Present. Cambridge: Harvard University Press, 1999.

About Spivak

Larson, Pier M. "Capacities and Modes of Thinking: Intellectual Engagements and Subaltern Hegemony in the Early History of Malagasy Christianity." *American Historical Review*, 102, no. 4 (1997): 969–1002.

*Morton, Stephen. *Gayatri Chakravorty Spivak.* London and New York: Routledge, 2003.

Sharpe, Jenny. "The Violence of Light in the Land of Desire; Or, How William Jones Discovered India." *Boundary 2*, 20, no. 1 (1993): 26–46.

Wakankar, Milind. "Body, Crowd, Identity: Genealogy of a Hindu Nationalist Ascetics." *Social Text* 45 (1995): 45–73.

Ward, Graham. *Theology and Contemporary Critical Theory.* 2nd ed. New York: St. Martin's Press, 2000.

Young, Robert. "Spivak: Decolonization, Deconstruction." In *White Mythologies: Writing History and the West.* London and New York: Routledge, 1990.

HAYDEN WHITE

Key Concepts

- fact as event under description
- metahistory
- history as interpretation
- tropology
- emplotment

Hayden White (1928–) is an American intellectual and cultural historian associated with a narrativist view of history. He earned his B.A. from Wayne State University and his Ph.D. from the University of Michigan in 1956. He held academic positions at the University of Rochester, University of California at Los Angeles, and Wesleyan University. In 1978 White became a professor in the History of Consciousness Program at the University of California at Santa Cruz. He was Presidential Professor of Historical Studies and is now University Professor Emeritus.

White approaches history from the perspective of language, suggesting that historical truth is always constructed through the narratives crafted by historians. Historical knowledge, therefore, is not simply the apprehension of an external reality, the truth of the past, but a product of the historian's discourse. White's work typically takes aim at binary oppositions that pretend to organize "reality" in a logical, objective way. From White's perspective, for example, the traditional opposition of history's facts to literature's fictions is a false one. Congruent with this view, White's own work is located at the intersection of historiography and literary theory and has had a significant impact on both areas.

White acknowledges that his theoretical positions owe a great deal to both older historians and philosophers, as well as to contemporaries such as Northrop Frye and Kenneth Burke. He is critical of positivist views of history that assert that objective observation of the past can uncover historical truths. Such thinking is predicated on binary oppositions such as objectivity/subjectivity, truth/falsity, and fact/fiction. Instead, White argues that historians do not discover the facts "out there" but rather construct the "truths" of the historical past through narratives and tropes. Facts and truths are, therefore, primarily the domain of language embedded in particular cultures. History, for White, is a discursive and rhetorical enterprise, not one of excavating objective, incontrovertible facts. White's ideas about historical discourse are contrary to traditional "realist" views of narrative that assume the posture of an omniscient narrator who tells a story characterized by uninterrupted flow. Such a narrative voice masks the usually fragmentary nature of historical sources and evidence. It creates the appearance of a complete and unambiguous story where none exists.

White describes a **"fact"** as **"an event under description."** By this he means that historical factuality is constructed by historians in language. The fact cannot be separated from its verbal description. For White, historical events belong to the domain of reality, but facts belong to historical discourse. White does not deny the reality of past events, but he argues that any claims made about what "really" happened—the facts—are made in narratives of those events. The historian has no access to past reality but only to discourses that assert facts about that past. In this sense, history is primarily a textual practice. When historians describe past events, they are really talking about how other narratives have told the story of the past.

It is here that White makes one of his most important claims, namely that the past does not exist apart from historical representations of it, and those historical representations—historical texts—are themselves "literary artifacts," that is, they too are part of history (see "Historical Text as Literary Artifact," in *Tropics of Discourse*). This claim is predicated, in part, on the observation that past events cannot be verified or "fact-checked." Differing interpretations of past events can be compared and critiqued to determine the most compelling narrative, but the events themselves are inaccessible. On this basis, White claims that history must attend to language, in particular to historical narratives, traditions of history writing, the genres used to narrate a persuasive historical discourse, and other linguistic and textual aspects of telling history. In other words, history must also be **metahistory**. That is, it must be self-conscious and self-critical about the presumptions and strategies it employs in order to make sense of the past.

One of White's operating assumptions is that any mode of human inquiry, including historical research, has political or ideological implications. In *The Content of the Form*, White notes that "narrative is not merely a neutral discursive form that may or may not be used to represent real events in their aspect as developmental processes but rather entails ontological and epistemic choices with distinct ideological and even specifically political implications" (*The Content of the Form*, p. ix). Historical narratives and other representations of the past are ideological because they promote a perspective on the past that cannot be

legitimated to "truth" or "objectivity" given the textual nature of the historiographical enterprise.

White's long career is punctuated by different phases of intellectual interest.
Of this work, arguably the most important to religious studies is White's work
on historical narrative as described in volumes such as *Metahistory: The
Historical Imagination in Nineteenth-Century Europe* (1973), *Tropics of Discourse:
Essays in Cultural Criticism* (1978), and *The Content of the Form: Narrative
Discourse and Historical Representations* (1987). The first two volumes articulate
White's arguments concerning historical narrative, discourse, and literary
tropes. The latter text deals with issues of historical representation and narrative
discourse.

In *Metahistory*, White uses structuralist ideas to understand the nature and
function of historical discourses. It is in this volume that White makes his
most important arguments about the narrative nature of history. White's narrativist philosophy of history sees the genre of literary narrative as central to
the historian's craft. Against the Aristotelian distinction of fact from fiction
that dominates contemporary historiography, White describes history as interpretation that takes the form of narrative. Here, White draws a distinction
between science as explanation and **history as interpretation**. Extending this
distinction, White wants to expose history's scientific conceit, that is, history's
traditional employment of explanatory models that are claimed to accurately
describe facts and external events in a logical and objective manner. Against
this conceit, he presents history as historical narrative, a mode of discourse
that sets forth interpretations of past events in a rhetorical manner. From this
perspective, explanation does not present us with objective historical verities,
but rather is best understood as a rhetorical device to persuade readers of the
truth of a particular view of past events (see "emplotment" below). White's
distinction between science and history can be charted as follows:

Science	History
models	tropes
explanation	interpretation
logic	rhetoric

White's theory of tropes (**tropology**) is central to arguments about historical
writing he expresses in *Metahistory*. A trope is usually understood as a figure
of speech, such as a metaphor. White, however, uses this term to refer to styles
or modes of thought used by historical narratives to craft their discursive
arguments. Through extensive research into the history of historiography,
he shows how historical texts from particular periods have in common the use
of certain tropes. For White, "troping is the soul of discourse" (*Tropics of*

Discourse, p. 2), and it is one of the chief tasks of the historian to identify what tropes are used and to uncover their ideological ramifications.

Following Giambattista Vico and Kenneth Burke, White sets forth a hierarchical typology based on four master tropes: metaphor, metonymy, synecdoche, and irony. He understands the first three tropes as "naïve" tropes, "since they can only be deployed in the belief in language's capacity to grasp the nature of things in figurative terms" (*Metahistory*, pp. 36–37). Irony, on the other hand, is self-reflexive about the problem of universal truth claims and is cognizant of the provisional nature of language. Thus White asserts that "Irony . . . represents a stage of consciousness in which the problematical nature of language itself has become recognized. It points to the potential foolishness of all linguistic characterizations of reality as much as to the absurdity of the beliefs it parodies" (*Metahistory*, p. 37).

White also discusses modes of **emplotment** utilized by historical discourse. Just as with literary narratives, historical narratives have a plot structure that is utilized by the historian to tell the story of past events. Using Frye, White identifies four primary modes of emplotment: romance, comedy, tragedy, and satire. These modes of emplotment in turn are connected to modes of explanation and ideological implications based on the work of Stephen Pepper and Karl Mannheim. White understands these levels of interpretation in historical narrative as "structurally homologous with one another" (*Tropics of Discourse*, p. 70). He represents this homological relationship as follows:

Mode of Emplotment	Mode of Explanation	Mode of Ideological implication
romance	idiographic	anarchist
comedy	organicist	conservative
tragedy	mechanistic	radical
satire	contextualist	liberal

White makes it clear that his interpretive typologies are not meant as rigid containers into which all texts must clearly find a place: "I do not suggest that these correlations necessarily appear in the work of a given historian; in fact, the tension at the heart of every historical masterpiece is created in part by a conflict between a given modality of emplotment or explanation and the specific ideological commitment of its author" (*Tropics of Discourse*, p. 70).

The narrative a historian creates from choices of plot, explanation, and ideology serves as an interpretation of past events. Historical interpretation has, according to White, at least three aspects: (1) the aesthetic (choice of narrative strategy); (2) the epistemological (choice of explanatory mode); and (3) the ethical (ideological choice). Historical discourse consists of these three interpretive aspects and thus presupposes a particular metahistory. "Every proper history presupposes a metahistory which is nothing but the web of commitments which the historian makes in the course of his interpretation on the aesthetic, cognitive, and ethical levels differentiated above" (*Tropics of Discourse*, p. 71). Thus, the issue for historians, according to White—and one that extends to the historian of religion—"is not, What are the facts? but rather, How are the facts to be described in order to sanction one mode of explaining them rather than another?" (*Tropics of Discourse*, p. 134).

White's theories on history as narrative pose intriguing questions for the academic study of religion to answer. To what extent are religion scholars aware of the assumptions and critical strategies that ground their studies? Like White's view of the historian narrating a history, is religion primarily a textual practice? Are religious traditions constructed by the narratives that religionists employ to talk about past events? Are there patterns of emplotment and ideology to religious texts, both those produced within religious traditions and those written by religion scholars? White breaks down the distinction between historical fact and literary fiction, rendering suspect the notion of clear textual genres. On this basis, what makes a text religious as opposed to historical or literary? White's theoretical perspective challenges us not only to self-reflexively consider our critical methods, but to think carefully about what counts as the textual, ritual, historical, and other objects of our study that we can claim these as proprietary to the discipline of religion. Attending to White's assertions seem all the more urgent when the Bible can be taught as literature and the novels of John Irving studied as religious texts.

Further Reading
By White

Metahistory: The Historical Imagination in Nineteenth-Century Europe. Baltimore: Johns Hopkins University Press, 1973.

*Tropics of Discourse: Essays in Cultural Criticism. Baltimore: Johns Hopkins University Press, 1978.

The Content of the Form: Narrative Discourse and Historical Representations. Baltimore: Johns Hopkins University Press, 1987.

About White

Bann, Stephen. "Analysing the Discourse of History." *Dalhousie Review* 64 (1984): 376–400.

Hammond, David M. "Hayden White: Meaning and Truth in History." *Philosophy & Theology* 8 (1994): 291–307.

Hutcheon, Linda. *A Poetics of Postmodernism: History, Theory, Fiction.* New York and London: Routledge, 1988.

*Jenkins, Keith. On "What Is History?": From Carr and Elton to Rorty and White. London and New York: Routledge, 1995.

Jenkins, Keith. "A Conversation with Hayden White." Literature and History 7 (1998): 68–82.

Konstan, David. "The Function of Narrative in Hayden White's Metahistory." CLIO 11, no.1 (1981): 65–78.

LaCapra, Dominick. Rethinking Intellectual History: Texts, Contexts, Language. Ithaca: Cornell University Press, 1983.

Rennie, Bryan. "Religion after Religion, History after History: Postmodern Historiography and the Study of Religions." Method and Theory in the Study of Religion 15, no. 3 (2003): 68–99.

RAYMOND WILLIAMS

Key Concepts

- Culture versus culture
- cultural studies
- ideal, documentary, and social culture
- the structure of feeling
- dominant, residual, and emergent aspects of history

Raymond Williams (1921–88) was a British literary theorist, novelist, leading Marxist, and one of the founders of cultural studies. He was born in Wales and raised in a working-class family (his mother was a housewife, his father a railway signalman). In 1939 he entered Cambridge University on a scholarship. There he studied literature and was a member of the Cambridge University Socialist Club. His studies were interrupted in 1942 when he was called to military duty, serving as a tank commander. After the war, Williams returned to Cambridge to finish his degree.

After graduating from Cambridge, he worked in the Adult Education Department at Oxford University for fifteen years, during which time he wrote two major works, *Culture and Society, 1780–1950* (1958) and *The Long Revolution* (1961). He joined the faculty at Cambridge University as a lecturer in English and drama in 1961 and remained there for the rest of his career.

Williams approached literature from an interdisciplinary Marxist perspective. He explored ways in which social class hierarchy was expressed in literature, usually to the advantage of the upper classes. He was also interested in ways that modes of communication are connected to the material conditions of a society. His theories, especially those on culture, have impacted other intellectual currents such as New Historicism, and are often associated with Hayden **WHITE**'s concept of metahistory and his focus on historiography as a form of interpretive narrative, which is never disinterested with regard to matters of social power.

Williams' ideas about culture are foundational for the field now known as cultural studies. In *The Long Revolution*, his second major theoretical writing, he explores conceptual issues connected with the term culture. He distinguishes between **Culture** (capital C) and **culture** (lowercase c). Culture (capital C) is a moral and aesthetic term originally conceived by English writers such as the Victorian poet and humanist Matthew Arnold and the modern literary critic F. R. Leavis. In their discourse, Culture means "high culture," that is, the sum total of civilization's greatest moral and aesthetic achievements. The not-so-hidden agenda of this idea of Culture, of course, is to assert and maintain social class—"high culture" and "high class" are synonymous. Against this view, Williams develops a concept of culture (lowercase c) in terms of the social. Here, culture is not composed exclusively of those ideas and achievements deemed to be the high points of civilization. Rather, culture includes all products of human activity, including language, social, political, and religious ideas and institutions, and other expressions both conceptual and material. In this sense, culture comprises all that humans create and enact in order to make sense of their existence.

It is this concept of culture that has served as the focal point for Williams' literary-cultural studies. By arguing that the concept of culture was irreducible to the products of an elite class, Williams helped create a new academic field—**cultural studies**—that examines the everyday life of nonelite groups.

This conception of culture as social is for Williams one of "three general categories in the definition of culture" (*The Long Revolution,* p. 57): the ideal, the documentary, and the social. **Ideal culture** refers to the concept of culture as a "state or process of human perfection" measured by absolute or universal standards. In this instance, cultural analysis "is essentially the discovery and description, in lives and works, of those values which can be seen to compose a timeless order, or to have permanent reference to the universal human condition" (*The Long Revolution*, p. 57). **Documentary culture** approaches culture as a documentary record, a repository for the artifacts of cultural achievements, including literature, arts, and philosophy. Here, "culture is the body of intellectual and imaginative work, in which, in a detailed way, human thought and experience are variously recorded" (*The Long Revolution*, p. 57). Finally, **social culture**, as mentioned earlier, focuses on culture not simply in terms of the artifacts and achievements of high, elite culture, but in terms of all the many ways that people conceive of and enact their lives. Thus culture encompasses the political, the religious, and the economic, as well as all modes of thought and practice by which people live in the world.

For Williams, thinking of culture in terms of this third definitional category, as social culture, breaks down distinctions between elite culture and the "popular" culture of the masses. Social culture claims that the products of elite culture are not to be valorized over the products of popular culture. All cultural products count as culture. In Williams' view, culture is not static, but rather is a process that on the one hand always asserts itself and acts on us, and on the other hand is constantly produced and changed by human beings. Cultural process flows both toward us and away from us. The idea of culture as social is meant to express this dynamism.

These three categories, or definitions, are to be understood, says Williams, as a whole and in terms of the interactions and relationships pertaining between these three aspects of culture: "However difficult it may be in practice, we have to try to see the process as a whole, and to relate our particular studies . . . to the actual and complex organization" (*The Long Revolution*, p. 60). One of the by-products of Williams's egalitarian, nonelitist view of culture was that he laid a foundation for the study of popular culture. Because all human products and practices are considered valuable and available for cultural analysis, forms of what we now refer to as popular culture—such as television, film, pop/rock music, sports, and Weblogs—are arguably more revealing about the nature of culture because it is in these aspects of culture that lived experiences of the nonelite are expressed. The products of high culture only tell us about elites; popular culture tells so much more because of its inclusivity. Williams studied popular culture in later works such as *Television: Technology and Cultural Form* (1974).

In his examination of culture, Williams pays considerable attention to what he calls the "**the structure of feeling**." According to Williams, a structure of feeling is the particular character and quality of a shared cultural sense. In general, Williams's notion of the structure of feeling refers to the lived experience of a people—or a generation of people—within particular cultural contexts. The lived experience includes the interaction between "official" culture—laws, religious doctrine, and other formal aspects of a culture—and the way that people live in their cultural context. The structure of feeling is what imbues a people with a specific "sense of life" and experience of community. It comprises the set of particular cultural commonalities shared by a culture despite the individual differences within it. As Williams notes, the sense of commonality is not necessarily shared throughout a culture, but is most likely the feeling of the dominant social group. This cultural, feeling is not typically expressed in any verbal, rational mode of discourse, though it can often be located in literary texts that reveal it only indirectly. Cultural analysis of the structure of feeling aims at uncovering how these shared feelings and values operate to help people make sense of their lives and the different situations in which the structure of feeling arises.

In *Marxism and Literature* (1977), Williams examines historiographical issues, arguing that the cultural analyst must recognize the complex interactions that occur within historical contexts and be careful to avoid privileging those dominant, empowered voices within it. In other words, rather than view history as a progression of nameable cultural periods—in which each period determines the one that follows—Williams wants to look at history through the lens of cultural struggle and resistance. To this end, he posits three terms "which recognize not only 'stages' and 'variations' but the internal dynamic relations of any actual process" (*Marxism and Literature*, p. 121). These are the "dominant," "residual," and "emergent" aspects of historical periods.

The **dominant** aspects of a historical period are the systems of thought and practice that dictate, or try to dictate, what can be thought and what can be done—that is, the assertion of dominant values, morality, and meanings. For Williams, the concept of the dominant is related to the concept of hegemony. The dominant is at once hegemonic, rigorously promoting the interests of the empowered and suppressing the interests of others. But the dominant does not stand uncontested. Williams reminds us that within any cultural context, the "effective dominant culture" is always under siege by alternative values, meanings, and practices that are not part of it. These alternatives and oppositions to the dominant culture can be found in "residual" and "emergent" forms.

The **residual** aspects of a historical period are past cultural formations. These old values and meanings may have once been dominant but have now been supplanted by the present dominant power. Aspects of these older cultural forms may still be active in the present, exerting pressure on the dominant forms, although they are generally subordinate to the dominant. In short, the residual can be incorporated into the dominant culture, and at the same time can have aspects which stand in opposition or as an alternative to that culture. Williams cites by way of example the residual nature of organized religion in contemporary English culture.

The **emergent** aspects of a historical period are those newly emerging values, meanings, and practices that adumbrate future cultural directions and put pressure on the existing dominant culture. Cultural forms can never be frozen by the dominant culture. Dominant culture is always undergoing opposition by these new cultural forms that threaten to replace the dominant.

Williams views these three relations of cultural process as the ground where struggles over dominance and resistance to hegemony are waged. Further, this tripartite view of historical process requires us to view culture as dynamic rather than static, and to be mindful of the interactions and cross-fertilization of these three aspects of cultural movement and change.

Williams' all-encompassing, nonelitist concept of culture and his development of a methodology for cultural studies have implications for religious studies. Above all, they have led to a shift in how religion is understood vis-à-vis culture. For Williams, and those who follow him in the field of cultural studies, religion is part of culture and must be studied along with all those other artifacts, activities, and beliefs by which people conceive of and enact their lives. By the same token, this conception of culture pushes religious studies to pay more attention to the banal, material, pedestrian aspects of a religious group's communal life. Too often scholarship interprets a religious group exclusively in terms of its established canons of scripture and thought—that is, in terms of the high, elite, dominant, literary aspects. Williams' approach to cultural studies encourages religionists to pay closer attention to other aspects—the popular, the everyday, the ordinary practices—that also play a central and vital role in a religious community's cultural life (see, for instance, Colleen McDannell's *Material Christianity: Religion and Popular Culture in America*).

Further Reading

By Williams

Culture and Society, 1780–1950. New York: Columbia University Press, 1958.

*The Long Revolution. Rev. ed. New York: Columbia University Press, 1966.

*Marxism and Literature. New York: Oxford University Press, 1977.

Problems in Materialism and Culture: Selected Essays. London and New York: Verso Books, 1980.

Keywords: A Vocabulary of Culture and Society. Rev. ed. New York: Oxford University Press, 1983.

The Raymond Williams Reader. Edited by John Higgins. Oxford: Blackwell Publishers, 2001.

About Williams

Eagleton, Terry, Ed. *Raymond Williams: Critical Perspectives*. Boston: Northeastern University Press, 1989.

Eldridge, J.E.T. *Raymond Williams: Making Connections*. London and New York: Routledge, 1994.

Higgins, John. *Raymond Williams: Literature, Marxism, and Cultural Materialism*. London and New York: Routledge, 1999.

*Inglis, Fred. *Raymond Williams*. New York: Routledge, 1995.

Light, Richard, and Louise Kinnaird. "Appeasing the Gods: Shinto, Sumo and 'True' Japanese Spirit." In *With God on Their Side: Sport in the Service of Religion*, edited by Tara Magdalinski and Timothy J. L. Chandler. London and New York: Routledge, 2002.

Masuzawa, Tomoko. "Culture." In *Critical Terms for Religious Studies*, edited by Mark C. Taylor. Chicago: University of Chicago Press, 1998.

McDannell, Colleen. *Material Christianity: Religion and Popular Culture in America*. New Haven: Yale University Press, 1998.

Prendergast, Christopher, Ed. *Cultural Materialism: On Raymond Williams*. Minneapolis: University of Minnesota Press, 1995.

SLAVOJ ŽIŽEK

Key Concepts

- authentic act
- agapé and Pauline Christianity
- Buddhism

Slavoj Žižek (1949–) is a senior researcher at the Institute of Sociology at University of Ljubljana, Slovenia, his hometown. He has also been a visiting professor at several American universities.

Following formal education, Žižek was initially unable to acquire an academic post (purportedly because he was not sufficiently Marxist) and resorted to working as a translator. In the 1970s he helped form the Ljubljana Lacanians, a small band of young intellectuals interested in **LACAN** (Žižek himself spent time in Paris working with both Lacan and Jacques Alain-Miller, Lacan's mentee and son-in-law). The group took over the journal *Problemi*. Žižek's own contributions to this journal are often parodies or literary hoaxes. Once he wrote an anonymous negative review of one of his own books on Lacan. This kind of playfulness continues in his later work.

Žižek is well known for his interpretations of popular culture, especially film and television (from Alfred Hitchcock's films to *The Matrix* to the Oprah Winfrey Show), in light of the theoretical canons of **MARX, LACAN**, and others. For this reason his work may appear to some as flippant and superficial. It is nothing of the sort. In all his work, Žižek seeks to develop a cultural theory that integrates psychoanalytic—especially Lacanian—conceptions of the subject with Marxian conceptions of ideology and political history. His description of his book series with Verso Press, *Wo es war* ("Where it was"), makes explicit the political wager involved in this intellectual venture: "the explosive combination of Lacanian psychoanalysis and Marxist tradition detonates a dynamic freedom that enables us to question the very presuppositions of the circuit of Capital." Žižek draws on Lacanian psychoanalysis to conceive of a subject who can live and act within the order of things in ways that expose and subvert the logic of late capitalism—blow its circuits—thereby opening new possibilities for being in the world in relation to others.

Žižek is critical of Judith **BUTLER**'s theory of subjectivity and social transformation, which he believes cannot break free from the stronghold of the symbolic order. For him, the subversive, gender-troubling performances that she calls for "ultimately support what they intend to subvert, since the very field of such 'transgressions' is already taken into account" by the symbolic order, which he describes as a "gargantuan symbolic matrix embodied in a vast set of ideological institutions, rituals and practices." This order "is a much too deeply rooted and 'substantial' entity to be effectively undermined by the marginal gestures of performative displacement" described by Butler (*The Ticklish Subject*, p. 208).

Žižek returns to Lacan to develop a theory of political action in which the subject, unable to locate a universal common ground on which to stand outside the constraints of the symbolic order, nevertheless can act in such a way as to break the "hypnotic force" of that order. Such an "**authentic act**" is not simply one of several options within the order of things but is in fact an act that exposes that order as a ruse and undermines its power over the subject, thus opening space for new kinds of social relations. In this way, Žižek insists on the possibility of a truly radical agency for subjects caught in the order of late capitalism, even while he acknowledges that such an agency cannot be solidly grounded. In a sense, the authentic act is a leap of faith, stepping off the false ground on which one stands without knowing exactly where one will land.

Some have seen psychoanalysis, including Lacanian psychoanalysis, as a basically conservative enterprise, in which the aim of analysis is to help the analysand reconcile to the symbolic order—to "work through" the in-breakings of the unconscious in such as way as to become happily integrated into the order of things, even if that order is in fact an illusion. To the contrary, Žižek insists that, for Lacan, psychoanalysis should enable the analysand to recognize that order as a "fake" and to break its hold on life (*The Fragile Absolute*, p. 114–15). In this psychoanalytic conception of the symbolic order and the subject's relation to it, Žižek finds an approach to the Marxian problem of how to break loose from the circuits of capitalism.

In *The Fragile Absolute or Why Is the Christian Legacy Worth Fighting for?* (2000) and in *On Belief* (2001), Žižek finds an affinity between his notion of the authentic act and Christian theology, especially the Apostle Paul's theology of the resurrection and especially *agapé*, "love" or "mercy." Christian *agapé*, as Žižek understands it in Paul's New Testament writings (especially I Corinthians 13), does not serve the symbolic order but is ally to his notion of the authentic act that exposes that order as a fake and breaks it open to otherness. "It is love itself that enjoins us to 'unplug' from the organic community into which we were born" (*The Fragile Absolute*, p. 121). The Christian gospel, as revelation, is a *traumatic event* against the Roman global empire and "pagan religion." Its trauma is located in its absolute claim that all people have access to the universal. That is, all people, regardless of class, gender, and ethnicity, and regardless of their place within the social and cosmic order posited by the empire and its religious ideology, have *direct* access to divine revelation, divine grace, and even adoption as children of God.

This is not to say that Žižek is on his way to conversion. His own rigorously Marxist and psychoanalytic commitments lead him to reject Christianity or any other theological appeal to faith in transcendence or redemption through divine atonement. Nonetheless, Žižek recognizes within this form of Pauline Christianity a certain radical orientation and potential in breaking the circuit of the Roman symbolic order.

Žižek finds this radical potential—this opening toward the authentic act that can break the hypnotic force of the symbolic—not only in Pauline Christianity but also in early **Buddhism** as expressed in the teachings of the Buddha.

> I can participate in this universal dimension [nirvana] *directly*, irrespective of my special place within the global social order. For that reason, Buddha's followers form a community of people who, in one way or another, have broken with the hierarchy of the social order and started to treat it as fundamentally *irrelevant*: In his choice of disciples, Buddha pointedly ignored castes and (after some hesitation, true) even sexual difference. (*The Fragile Absolute*, p. 122)

Privileging social outcasts as exemplary, the early communities around Jesus and the Buddha worked, stresses Žižek, to suspend established social hierarchy, thereby "unplugging" or "uncoupling" from its circuitry. Here, then, as in Pauline Christian theology, he recognizes a certain affinity with his own interest in concocting an "explosive combination" of Marxism and Lacanian psychoanalysis thought that "enables us to question the very presuppositions of the circuit of Capital."

Further Reading
By Žižek

The Ticklish Subject: The Absent Centre of Political Ontology. London and New York: Verso Books, 1999.

Enjoy Your Symptom! Jacques Lacan in Hollywood and Out. New York and London: Routledge, 2001.

On Belief. London and New York: Routledge, 2001.

The Fragile Absolute or, Why Is the Christian Legacy Worth Fighting For? London and New York: Verso Books, 2000.

About Žižek

Hart, William D. "Slavoj Žižek and the Imperial/Colonial Model of Religion," in *Nepantla: Views from South* 3:3 (2002) <muse.jhu.edu/journals/nepantla>.

Pizzino, Christopher. "A Legacy of Freaks." *Postmodern Culture* 12, no. 2 (2002). <muse.jhu.edu/journals/postmodern_culture>.

Santner, Eric. *On the Psychotheology of Everyday Life*. Chicago: University of Chicago Press, 2001.

Thomassen, Lasse. "The Politics of Lack," *Postmodern Culture* 11, no. 3 (2001). <muse.jhu.edu/journals/postmodern_culture>.